Longman Handbooks for Language Teachers

Susan Halliwell

Teaching English in the Primary Classroom

Longman

Pearson Education Limited
Edinburgh Gate, Harlow,
Essex CM20 2JE, England
and Associated Companies throughout the world

www.longman.com

Distributed in the United States of America by
Addison Wesley Longman, New York

First published 1992
Eighteenth impression 2008

ISBN 978-0-582-07109-4

BRITISH LIBRARY CATALOGUING IN PUBLICATION DATA
Halliwell, Susan
    Teaching English in the Primary
    Classroom. – (Longman Handbooks for Language Teachers
    Series)
    I. Title   II. Series
    372.6521044

LIBRARY OF CONGRESS CATALOGING IN PUBLICATION DATA
Halliwell, Susan.
    Teaching English in the primary classroom / Susan Halliwell.
        p.   cm. – (Longman handbooks for language teachers)
    ISBN 0-582-07019-7
    1. English language–Study and teaching (Primary) – Foreign
speakers.   I. Title.   II. Series
PE1128.A2H287   1992   91–37793
428.2'4–dc20   CIP

Set in 10/12 pt Monophoto Times
by Servis Filmsetting, Ltd, Manchester
Printed in Malaysia, PJB

Acknowledgements
We are grateful to the following for their permission to
reproduce copyright photographs:
Ed & Trudie Barnes for page 82 (left, right). Trudie Barnes &
Lisa Howard for page 82 (middle). Malcolm Booker for
page 103. Susan Halliwell for pages 99, 123, 124.

Longman Handbooks for Language Teachers

The Practice of English Language Teaching New Edition – Jeremy Harmer
An Introduction to English Language Teaching – John Haycraft
Teaching Oral English New Edition – Donn Byrne
Communication in the Classroom – edited by Keith Johnson and Keith Morrow
Teaching English Through English – Jane Willis
Teaching English with Video – Margaret Allan
Using Computers in the Language Classroom – Christopher Jones and Sue Fortescue
Teaching English Pronunciation – Joanne Kenworthy
Writing English Language Tests New Edition – J.B. Heaton
Teaching Writing Skills New Edition – Donn Byrne
Teaching Listening – Mary Underwood
Teaching on Holiday Courses – Nick Dawson
Process Writing – Ron White and Valerie Arndt
Teaching Literature – Ronald Carter and Michael N. Long
Teaching English in the Primary Classroom – Susan Halliwell

Contents

Acknowledgement

We all learn from each other. I would like to
acknowledge my enormous debt to all the
children and teachers who have helped me
with these ideas and who will recognise their
contributions in these materials.

PART I

Priorities and practical considerations

Introduction

Working with young language learners in the primary classroom can be both a rewarding and a demanding experience. To make the most of that experience for both learners and teachers we need to be very clear what it is we are trying to do. We must try to identify what learning a language in school demands from young children and what it can offer them. We should also acknowledge what the implications of those demands and needs are for the teachers.

This section of the book starts with the learners themselves. It shows how they bring with them to the classroom existing skills and instincts which help them to learn a new language. It also discusses how those skills and instincts form the foundation for our priorities with young learners. Finally it relates these ideals and ideas to the daily practical realities of the classroom. The first section ends with suggestions for language activities based on the principles and practical considerations of the first three chapters.

1 Working with young language learners.
2 Identifying priorities and their implications.
3 Being realistic.

Practical Activities 1.

1

Working with young language learners

Young children do not come to the language classroom empty-handed. They bring with them an already well-established set of instincts, skills and characteristics which will help them to learn another language. We need to identify those and make the most of them. For example, children:

– are already very good at interpreting meaning without necessarily understanding the individual words;
– already have great skill in using limited language creatively;
– frequently learn indirectly rather than directly;
– take great pleasure in finding and creating fun in what they do;
– have a ready imagination;
– above all take great delight in talking!

How does each of these qualities help a child in the foreign language classroom and how can the teacher build on them?

1.1
Children's ability to grasp meaning

We know from experience that very young children are able to understand what is being said to them even before they understand the individual words. Intonation, gesture, facial expressions, actions and circumstances all help to tell them what the unknown words and phrases probably mean. By understanding the message in this way they start to understand the language. In later life we all maintain this first source of understanding alongside our knowledge of the language itself. It remains a fundamental part of human communication.

Children come to primary school with this ability already highly developed. They continue to use it in all their school work. For example, even though their mother tongue skills are already well established, they may well find it difficult to follow purely verbal instructions and information. When this happens, or sometimes simply out of laziness or inattention, children will tend to rely on their ability to 'read' the general message. In fact we can see this

3

happening most clearly when they get it wrong! More importantly, particularly in terms of language development, their message-interpreting skill is part of the way they learn new words, concepts and expressions in their mother tongue as their language expands to meet the new challenges of school.

So when children encounter a new language at school, they can call on the same skill to help them interpret the new sounds, new words and new structures. We want to support and develop this skill. We can do this by making sure we make full use of gesture, intonation, demonstration, actions and facial expressions to convey meaning parallel to what we are saying. The account in *Practical Activities 2* of the science lesson taught in English shows in detail how you can do this. At the same time, we must also try not to undermine the children's willingness to use the skill. As we shall see in Chapter 2, this can happen when we try to 'pin down' understanding too precisely.

Alongside this ability to perceive meaning, children also show great skill in producing meaningful language from very limited resources. This too will help them when they encounter a new language and is therefore something else we want to build on.

1.2 Children's creative use of limited language resources

In the early stages of their mother tongue development children excel at making a little language go a long way. They are creative with grammatical forms. They are also creative with concepts. The four-year-old British child who said 'don't unring' when she wanted to tell a telephone caller to wait, was using her existing knowledge of the way the negative prefix works in order to create a meaning she needed. Similarly another four year old was showing the same kind of creativity, this time with concepts, when he wanted the light put on. What he actually said was 'Switch off the dark. I don't like the dark shining.' Children also create words by analogy, or they even invent completely new words which then come into the family vocabulary.

This phenomenon is fundamental to language development. We see it in all children acquiring their mother tongue. We also know it in ourselves as adults when we are using another language. Sometimes, for example, we don't know the word or the grammatical structure for what we want to say. So we find other ways of conveying the meaning. Sometimes we just make up words or even just say words from our mother tongue in a foreign accent. We stretch our resources to the limit. In the process, we may well produce temporarily inexact and sometimes inept language, but we usually manage to communicate. In doing so we are actually building up our grasp of the language because we are *actively recombining* and *constructing* it for ourselves.

This process would appear to be a very deep-rooted human instinct. It actually occurs in the language classroom even without our help. For example, it occurs naturally when the need to communicate has been temporarily intensified by some activity which generates real interaction or calls on the imagination. In order to make the most of the creative language skill the children bring with them, we therefore have to provide them with occasions when:

– the urge to communicate makes them find *some* way of expressing themselves;
– the language demanded by the activity is unpredictable and isn't just asking the children to repeat set phrases, but is encouraging them to construct language actively for themselves.

That is why games are so useful and so important. It is not just because they are fun. It is partly because the fun element creates a desire to communicate and partly because games can create unpredictability.

If we acknowledge the need for unpredictability, it follows that in addition to occasions when the children practise learnt dialogues or other specific language items under close teacher guidance, there will also need to be occasions when we set up an activity and then leave the children to get on with it. This obviously raises questions about mistakes and correction but, as the next chapter shows, there are good reasons why we must allow the children opportunities to make mistakes. In fact, if children are impatient to communicate they probably will make *more* not *fewer* mistakes.

The desire to communicate also ties in with the next capacity that children bring with them to the classroom, namely their aptitude for indirect learning.

1.3 Children's capacity for indirect learning

Even when teachers are controlling an activity fairly closely, children sometimes seem to notice something out of the corner of their eye and to remember it better than what they were actually supposed to be learning. At times this can be a frustrating experience for the teacher but this capacity too can be turned to our advantage in the language classroom. It is part of the rather complex phenomenon of indirect learning.

Language activities which involve children in guessing what phrase or word someone has thought of are very good examples of this phenomenon in action. As far as the children are concerned, they are not trying to learn phrases: they are concentrating on trying to guess right. However, by the time they have finished the repeated guessing, they will have confirmed words and structures they only half knew at the beginning. They will have got the phrases firmly into their minds. They will probably even have adjusted their pronunciation. Guessing is actually a very powerful way of learning phrases and structures, but it is *indirect* because the mind is engaged with the task and is not focusing on the language. The process relates very closely to the way we develop our mother tongue. We do not consciously set out to learn it. We *acquire* it through continuous exposure and use.

Both conscious direct learning and subconscious indirect learning, or 'acquisition', are going to help someone internalise a new language. Experience tells us that we all seem to have something of both systems in us. It will depend on a mixture of intellectual development, temperament and circumstance whether we are more inclined to use one system rather than the other. In practical terms each system has its contribution to make. Conscious direct learning seems to encourage worked-out accuracy. Unconscious indirect learning, or acquisition, encourages spontaneous and therefore more fluent use. Ideally we want both accuracy and fluency to develop. So in the classroom we need to provide scope for both systems to operate. Within our lessons there will therefore need to be times for conscious focus on language forms *and* times for indirect learning with its focus on making meaning. There will be times for both precision *and* for rough and ready work. You may also notice that in your class you have children who are temperamentally more inclined to operate in one way than the other. In all aspects of life there are people who like to get everything sorted out and others who like to 'muddle through'. The children who like to get on with something no matter how it comes out will need

5

encouragement to work at conscious accuracy, and others who are keen to be precise will need encouragement to risk getting things wrong sometimes in order to communicate. We must be clear in our own minds which we are trying to encourage at any given moment and must also make it clear to the children in the way we set up activities what it is we are asking them to do. This is because each of the processes can easily get in the way of the other.

In general terms, however, it is probably true to say that at primary school level the children's capacity for conscious learning of forms and grammatical patterns is still relatively undeveloped. In contrast, all children, whether they prefer to 'sort things out' or 'muddle through', bring with them an enormous instinct for indirect learning. If we are to make the most of that asset we need to build on it quite deliberately and very fully.

For this reason, we can see why it is a good idea to set up real tasks in the language classroom if we can. Real tasks, that is to say worthwhile and interesting things to do which are not just language *exercises*, provide the children with an occasion for real language use, and let their subconscious mind work on the processing of language while their conscious mind is focused on the task. We can also see again why games are more than a fun extra. They too provide an opportunity for the real using and processing of language while the mind is focused on the 'task' of playing the game. In this way, games are a very effective opportunity for indirect learning. They should therefore not be dismissed as a waste of time. Nor should we regard them just as something we can introduce as a filler for the end of the lesson or as a reward for 'real work'. They *are* real work. They are a central part of the process of getting hold of the language. This is perhaps just as well because children have a very strong sense of play and fun.

1.4 Children's instinct for play and fun

Children have an enormous capacity for finding and making fun. Sometimes, it has to be said, they choose the most inconvenient moments to indulge it! They bring a spark of individuality and of drama to much that they do. When engaged in guessing activities, for example, children nearly always inject their own element of drama into their hiding of the promptcards and their reactions to the guesses of their classmates. They shuffle their cards ostentatiously under the table so that the others can't see. They may utter an increasingly triumphant or smug 'No!' as the others fail to guess. Or when they are doing the 'telepathy' exercise suggested on page 61 they enter into the spirit of the event. They know perfectly well it isn't 'real' but it doesn't stop them putting effort and drama into it. They stare hard at the rest of the class, they frown or they glower. Here, as in the guessing activities, their personalities emerge, woven into the language use. In this way, they make the language their own. That is why it is such a very powerful contribution to learning.

Similarly, no matter how well we explain an activity, there is often someone in the class who produces a version of their own! Sometimes it is better than the teacher's original idea. Some of the activities in *Practical Activities 1* have already been changed in this way from their original form by the children who have used them. One example of how children can produce something better than the teacher's own idea comes from a class of nine to ten year olds. They were doing an activity which asked them to follow directions round a map in order to check true/false statements about the location of shops. The cards and maps they were using had been clipped together with a paper clip. One pair proceeded to 'drive' the paper clip round the map each time they traced the route. They made appropriate cornering noises as they turned left or right, and reversed with much vocal squealing of brakes when they went wrong! The teacher's first reaction was to tell them not to be silly. Second thoughts suggested that by translating understanding into physical reaction they had thought up a much more powerful way of giving meaning to the phrases 'turn left/turn right, take the second turning on the left/right' etc. than the teacher could have created. It was also powerful because they had thought of it for themselves.

In this way, through their sense of fun and play, the children are living the language for real. Yet again we can see why games have such a central role to play. But games are not the only way in which individual personalities surface in the language classroom. There is also the whole area of imaginative thinking.

1.5
The role of imagination

Children delight in imagination and fantasy. It is more than simply a matter of enjoyment, however. In the primary school, children are very busing making sense of the world about them. They are identifying pattern and also deviation from that pattern. They test out their versions of the world through fantasy and confirm how the world actually is by imagining how it might be different. In the language classroom this capacity for fantasy and imagination has a very constructive part to play.

Language teaching should be concerned with real life. But it would be a great pity if we were so concerned to promote reality in the classroom that we forgot that reality for children includes imagination and fantasy. The act of fantasising, of imagining, is very much an authentic part of being a child. So, for example, describing an imaginary monster with five legs, ten pink eyes and a very long tongue may not involve actual combinations of words that they would use about things in real life, but recombining familiar words and ideas to create a monster is a very normal part of a child's life. Similarly, claiming a dinosaur in a list of pets is hardly real in purist terms but perfectly normal for a nine year old with a sense of the absurd. Children's books reflect this kind of fantasising with titles such as *The Tiger Who Came To Tea* or *The Giant Jam Sandwich*.

If we accept the role of the imagination in children's lives we can see that it provides another very powerful stimulus for real language use. We need to find ways of building on this factor in the language classroom too. We want to stimulate the children's creative imagination so that they want to use the language to share their ideas. For example, they can draw and describe the monster that lives down the hole on the next page. What does it eat? What does it look like? How old is it? (A chance at last to use numbers above eleven!) They will no doubt want to tell their friends about the monster they have drawn. Children like talking.

1.6
The instinct for interaction and talk

Of all the instincts and attributes that children bring to the classroom this is probably the most important for the language teacher. It is also the most obvious, so there is no need to labour the point. Let us just say that this particular capacity can surface unbidden and sometimes unwanted in all classrooms. Its persistence and strength is very much to our advantage in the primary language classroom. It is one of the most powerful motivators for using the language. We are fortunate as language teachers that we can build on it. Even so, you will sometimes hear teachers object – 'But I can't do pairwork with this class. They will keep talking to each other!' Far from being a good reason for not doing pairwork with them, this is a very good reason why we should. Children need to talk. Without talking they cannot become good at talking. They can learn *about* the language, but the only way to learn to *use* it *is* to use it. So our job is to make sure that the desire to talk is working *for* learning not *against* learning. *Practical Activities 1* gives detailed activities which do just this.

This chapter has identified some of the skills and instincts a young child brings to learning a foreign language at school. By saying we wish to build on these we are already beginning to describe the language classroom we want to see and the kind of things we want to do. In other words, our goals and priorities are beginning to emerge. The next chapter looks at those goals and priorities in more detail and explores their practical implications.

2

Identifying priorities and their implications

One of the great moments in the foreign language classroom is when a child makes a joke. The child who insisted with a grin that he had 'one and half' (*sic*) brothers and when questioned about the half by the puzzled teacher, said, 'Very small' (showing baby size with his hands), had broken through a crucial barrier. He had made the language *his*, a tool for what he wanted to say. He was using half-known bits of the language to give shape to the thoughts going through his mind. We have heard a great deal about authenticity. *This* is the greatest authenticity of them all. This small and apparently trivial incident encapsulates what we are trying to achieve. We want our learners to want to and dare to use the language for their own purposes. We want them to use it accurately if possible, inaccurately if necessary, but above all we want them to *make it theirs*.

We can't sit around in our classrooms waiting for jokes to happen, but there are other ways in which teachers can help the children to make the language theirs. You can give priority to:

- basing your teaching approaches on the natural capacities and instincts children bring to the classroom;
- developing a positive response to languages and to language learning (attitude goals) as well as to what they learn (content goals);
- making sure that you set up various forms of *real language use* as part of the *process* of learning, and not just as the intended *product*.

Chapter 1 looked at the practical significance of the first of these priorities. This chapter will look in detail at attitude goals and at real language use. Your own priorities may well be different. There are few, if any, absolute rights and wrongs in the classroom. However, by identifying one coherent set of priorities in this way, the intention is to allow you to identify and clarify your own priorities and to provide you with some basis for comparison. If each of us is clear about our priorities and their practical implications, we can avoid the situation where we actually teach in a way that undermines what it is we are trying to do.

2.1
Giving high priority to attitude goals

Most syllabuses or language programmes identify two sorts of goals. These can very roughly be described as the 'content goals' and the 'attitude goals'. The main difference between primary school and secondary school language work is the balance between these two kinds of goals. It is therefore worth looking more closely at them.

Content goals are concerned with the elements of language and ways in which they are used. The parts of syllabuses which describe content goals are usually arranged in one of the following ways.

- **Structures**: programmes are set out in terms of grammatical structures like *the present continuous* or *negatives*. Sometimes they just list the structures themselves, e.g. *I like swimming/dancing/reading* or *I don't/can't/won't*.
- **Topics and situations**: in these programmes the work is arranged according to topics or situations like *the family*, *at the supermarket*. Sometimes the items to be covered are grouped according to whether they demand speaking, listening, reading or writing.
- **Functions**: here the focus is on what the learner can use the language for, so the things to be covered are listed under headings like *expressing likes/ dislikes/preferences*, *asking and giving directions*, *expressing the future*.

Your own syllabus may reflect any one of these approaches. In fact, many syllabuses adopt a pragmatic combination of all three. However, whatever form your syllabus takes, whatever particular language-teaching ideology it reflects, these kinds of goals are concerned with the elements of the language and how the learners put them together to use them. That is to say, they are in essence *content* goals. There is, however, another very significant aspect to the syllabus, namely the *attitude* goals.

Good syllabuses are not just concerned with content. They are also concerned with attitude and response. Sometimes these goals are assumed. Sometimes they are written. If they are written into the syllabus you will find phrases like:

- pleasure and confidence in exploring language;
- willingness to 'have a go';
- the children should want to and dare to communicate.

In other words, in addition to having goals which are concerned with the actual language elements the children learn, we also have goals which relate to the kind of learning experiences we set up and the relationships and atmosphere of the language classroom.

The balance between the attitude goals and content goals shifts as a child moves through the education system. In the later stages of a child's education the content goals begin to dominate. Secondary teaching does not, or should not, lose sight of the attitude goals, but as the formal examination system approaches, priorities lie very much with the content, i.e. the language items to be mastered.

Primary language work, in contrast, can give emphasis to the attitude goals. It should not lose sight of the content goals but should at the same time give clear priority to promoting the attitudes and responses mentioned above, i.e. confidence, willingness to 'have a go', risk taking. At primary school we have more freedom to do this because most of us are not yet too tightly constrained by the content focus of the public examinations system. It can also be argued that we have a *responsibility* to give high priority to the attitude goals at primary level. After all, if we do not establish risk taking, confidence and general goodwill towards language learning at this early stage, our colleagues at secondary level will have a very difficult task ahead of them. In all subjects, of course, not just in foreign languages, the learners' response to the work is central to their later progress. In languages, however, this aspect is particularly crucial. This is because of the special nature of language.

2.2 The special nature of language

A language isn't just a 'subject' in the sense of a package of knowledge. It is not just a set of information and insights. It is a fundamental part of being human. In fact some people see it as *the* fundamental part of being human. It is, of course, perfectly possible to treat a language as if it were a free-standing package of information, i.e. to observe it, to analyse it and to fit together examples of how others use it. It is even possible to use this analysis and working out as the way to learn to use the language ourselves. Many of us who are now teachers first learnt a foreign language that way. For some it leads to success. But it is a very abstract process and experience has shown that it does not appeal to everyone. To learn to use a language at all well for ourselves rather than for textbook purposes, most of us have to become involved in it as an experience. We have to make it a human event not just a set of information. We do this by using it for real communication, for genuinely giving and receiving real messages.

As we have already seen, giving and receiving real messages in the early stages of learning a language, whether it is our mother tongue or a second language, involves using limited resources creatively. So we can see why attitudes such as confidence and risk taking have a central role in language learning. The important point to remember is that the attitude goals are not just there in order to motivate the children to accept the content. They are far more crucial than that. We need them in our language teaching because they are a key part of the *process* by which language develops.

This all sounds very important but the big question is, of course, how it affects what we actually do in the classroom. Is it difficult to make attitude goals a high priority? If we do, how does it show? The answer to the first question is 'No'. If you know that that is what you want to do, it is not difficult. The answer to the second question is that giving a high priority to attitude goals will show in the kind of interaction set up between teachers and learners and between learners themselves. Two examples will demonstrate this:

– the checking of understanding;
– the correction of mistakes.

2.3
The significance of the way we check understanding

Unless we are true bilinguals, most of us operate in a foreign language by taking the risk of operating on partial information. We may well not understand completely what has been said to us, but we are usually willing to guess the bits we don't understand or to operate as if we do understand everything. In classrooms however, we often hear teachers checking the meaning of almost every word of English as they go along. They perhaps say one sentence in English and then translate it back into the mother tongue. Or perhaps they get the children to translate it. They keep asking 'Do you understand?'

This happens from the best of motives. Ironically, the teacher wants to make sure that the children are secure and confident! What ultimately happens is the reverse. By constant checking in this way the teachers are implying that they expect the children to understand every little bit they hear. From that it follows that the children begin to think that they will not be able to understand at all unless they *do* understand every little bit. They will also come to believe that they have not understood unless they can give an exact mother tongue equivalent. In fact, they are unlikely to be able to understand everything. Nor do they need to. Nor will they always be able to give a mother tongue equivalent for something they have understood. Even in our mother tongue we do not understand every little bit. We deal with whole messages. As you are reading this you are not stopping over every word. If you did slow right down like that, the meaning would begin to disintegrate. As primary teachers you will see this happening when children at an early stage of reading are reading aloud. As they concentrate on each single word in turn, the meaning disappears both for them and for the listener. Constant explicit checking in the foreign language has the same effect.

Of course, we still need to check their understanding somehow, but we do not have to draw their attention to the fact that we are doing so. We can check by watching what they do, watching their faces. Teachers do this all the time anyway. If we can see that they do not understand, perhaps by the look on their faces, perhaps by the way they are sitting, or more obviously by the fact that they do not do what we are expecting, then we can rephrase the words or show them again what we mean before the temporary lack of understanding becomes critical.

2.4
The significance of the way we treat mistakes

Giving priority to attitude goals in principle also affects our practice in another way, namely the way we treat mistakes. Real conversation does not wait for us to work out everything exactly. Even if we get our first sentence out reasonably well, there is no guarantee that the other speaker will 'play by the rules' and answer as we expect or in words and phrases we know. So real communication demands risk taking. Trying out knowledge when it is still only half formed, as in the joke at the beginning of this chapter, is part of the process of shaping it up fully. Without risks and mistakes we could not learn anything.

Most children arrive at school with their confidence still intact. They do not expect to be able to do everything immediately, but they assume they can do anything eventually. In other words, for children mistakes and failures are frustrating rather than humiliating. They are a normal part of learning to do something. After all, nearly everything they do takes many attempts and takes a long time and even then is frequently still not quite right. Unfortunately, one of the things children soon begin to pick up at school is the idea that mistakes are in some way 'bad'. They begin to be embarrassed and upset when they have difficulty. They sometimes hide this embarrassment by laughing when others get something wrong. Then they start to protect themselves from disappointment and the scorn of others in turn by avoiding situations where they themselves might get things wrong. This shows in various ways. For example, a child does not attempt answers or gives up very easily. Or sometimes we have children in our classes who want to check every single stage of their work with the teacher. This is, of course, an oversimplified description of a complex process, but it is one which teachers of young children often see and one which we must do our best to counteract.

There is a very practical implication for language teachers here. It means that the way we correct mistakes is going to be very important. Teachers can inadvertently contribute to the undermining and inhibiting process. For example, in language classes you will often see teachers correcting every single mistake of pronunciation and grammar. By demanding correction or repetition of a word that has just been said, they break into the child's attempt to construct a whole meaning. (To remind yourself how disruptive this is, get a friend to correct your pronunciation of every third word as you try to tell them what you have been doing during the day.) Something similar often happens with written work too. If it always comes back completely covered in corrections of the smallest detail, it can destroy the urge to commit anything to paper at all and certainly to risk something of your own.

Again this constant, overcareful, overdetailed correction happens with the best of intentions. Teachers want children to get things right. But if we have to get everything perfect we will never try anything. Luckily, communication does not demand one hundred per cent accuracy. For example, we can understand someone else speaking our language even if they have a fairly strong accent. Sometimes even in our own language we don't get our words or structures quite right. If we listen carefully to native speakers, we find that they say some very odd and very ungrammatical things. But that doesn't seem to stop us understanding and communicating.

This is not to deny the value of correction. It is, however, arguing that constant correction is undermining. There will, of course, be times in lessons when the teacher is concentrating on accuracy. However, there will also be other times in lessons when you will be trying to encourage fluency. Correction is vital in the first and potentially destructive in the second. If one of our priorities is to get children to have confidence, we have to know this and to distinguish these occasions accordingly. This will also help us to deal with a practical problem. If we are expected to correct everything the children say, then pairwork with forty children in the room becomes laughingly impossible. If, on the other hand, we know that there are certain activities in which we actually wish to allow for mistakes, then suddenly pairwork becomes much more manageable. We will still want to move round the class to check that most of the children are getting it reasonably right. We will also want to help individual children, or to offer occasional correction. Correction is not forbidden! However, we do not have to run round the room frantically trying to hear everything everybody says.

So we can see in these two examples that giving high priority to attitude goals is not just an abstract matter of principle. It has very clear practical implications for the classroom. We will now look at some of the practical implications of the other main focus of this chapter. How does it show if we give priority to real language use?

The truest form of real language use is to use the language being learnt as a tool for other tasks and other learning. This is what happens in bilingual education where children are educated entirely in a language other than their mother tongue. Another, but more modest form of real language use, is provided by teaching other subject topics and lessons in the target language. Chapter 6 suggests in detail how this can be done. Meanwhile, however, it is also possible to create real language use in more typical language lessons, using a typical textbook.

– You can look for ways of making language exercises into real exchanges.
– You can teach language lessons through the medium of the target language itself.

2.5 Making language exercises into real exchanges

Wanting to communicate means having a good reason for doing so. We are not very interested in telling someone something they already know. Similarly, we do not particularly want to be told something we can already see for ourselves. There is only a limited point in saying 'She is wearing a green dress,' if both the child and the teacher can see the same picture. In this situation the only reason for the child to make the statement is to check it or to please the teacher. Pleasing the teacher has its limitations as a motivating factor! We have a much stronger reason for communicating if we are offering or seeking information that is not already shared.

There are plenty of classroom activities which provide an extremely useful combination of real communication and quite deliberate rehearsal of a clearly identified set of fairly restricted material. They can involve any of the four skills of listening, speaking, reading and writing, but their biggest contribution at primary level is probably in the field of spoken interaction between children. Because the range of language items can be limited without destroying the element of real communication, the teacher can leave the children talking to each other without fear that the need to communicate will lead them to lapse totally into the mother tongue. That is why so-called 'information gap' activities continue to be so popular in the language classroom. Look at the following example. It is a 'describe and arrange' activity.

The pair of children sit opposite each other and erect a visual barrier so that neither can see what the other is doing. The barrier can be a textbook or two flat folders propped against each other and held with a paper clip. Each child has the same base picture sheet and a set of small pictures of items relating to it. In this case, it is an outline of a room and various furniture items to arrange in it.

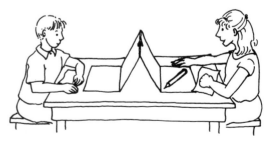

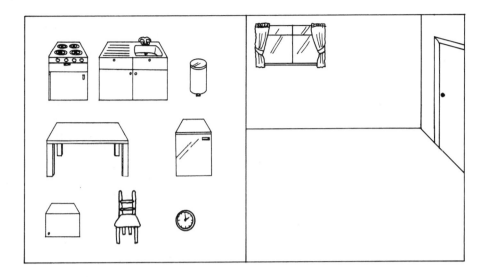

Child A starts to arrange the furniture in the room. By cooperative question/
answer exchanges the pair have to get child B's furniture arranged identically
but they may not look at each other's pictures. So B can ask 'Where is the
chair?' or, better, 'Is the chair next to the door?' which introduces an element of
guessing. You will find that this kind of 'describe and arrange' activity is one
where children take imaginative liberties. They arrange fridges on roofs and
bicycles in the bathroom in order to confuse matters by being unpredictable.

There is real communication here in the sense that one of the participants
has information that is needed by the other. At the same time, however, the
linguistic demands are realistically contained. The elements may be recombined
by the children to suit their own purposes, but the language being used is
limited to a few objects and a set of prepositions which will have been practised
thoroughly beforehand. There is thus some room for unpredictability and
choice within the security of a limiting framework.

**2.6
Teaching
language lessons
in the target
language**

The advantage of this second form of real language use in the classroom is that
it contributes to the learning process by:

- encouraging the children to trust their instinct to predict meaning in spite of
  limited linguistic understanding;
- providing an element of indirect learning in that the children are not
  concentrating on learning what they are listening to but the brain is
  processing it nonetheless;
- confirming that language is something you actually use 'for real' and not just
  something you do exercises and games in;
- increasing the amount of exposure the children get to the language, while still
  remaining within the fairly predictable and narrowly focused limits of
  classroom talk.

It is because classroom talk is relatively limited in this way that it is possible to
teach a whole lesson almost entirely in the target language on the basis of a
surprisingly small number of phrases and structures. Even so, most of us worry
initially that our own grasp of the foreign language is not good enough to do

15

this. We also worry that the children will not understand and will behave badly. There are two things worth saying here. First of all, you do not have to find the foreign language equivalent for 'What on earth do you think you are doing punching Thomas like that?' It works just as effectively to say in the target language 'Don't do that!' or even just 'No!' Secondly, children, as we have already seen, respond very well to context and facial expression. This was shown very clearly by the two small English children whose teacher finally lost patience with their misbehaviour and said very angrily in Spanish that if they misbehaved again she'd murder them. At this point, one child turned to the other and said, 'I don't know what she said, but if we do it again she'll kill us!'

Even on less dramatic occasions, you can actually get a very long way with 'Yes', 'No', 'Like this', 'Do this' and 'Don't do that!' With a little more than that you can use simple target language to set up really quite complicated activities. Here is an example. On page 87 there is a 'paired reading' activity. Each pair or group of children has two sets of cards. One set has words or phrases. The other set has pictures or diagrams. The idea is that the children have to read the phrases and match them up with the pictures. If the teacher was using the mother tongue, the explanation would sound something like this.

> 'Spread the word cards out face down on the table and put the picture cards in a pile face down. The first player takes a picture card from the top of the pile and chooses a word card from the cards spread out face down on the table. If they match, the player keeps the pair. If they don't match, the picture card is replaced at the bottom of the pile and the word card is put face down again where it came from. The winner is the person who collects the most pairs.'

However, trying out this activity on in-service courses for teachers has shown that after such a mother-tongue explanation, there are often still a considerable number of people who are not sure what to do. So there are two things to note.

- The words on their own are not enough to carry the meaning. Even when we understand each word the total sense seems to slip past.
- Teaching in the target language must very decidedly *not* take the form of simply giving the target language equivalent of the mother-tongue explanation above. Not only does that ask a great deal of the teacher's own language. It would also only compound the incomprehension.

The thing to remember yet again is that we have systems other than words for carrying meaning. This does not mean that the teacher has to become a non-stop and elaborate mime artist! It simply means that we deliberately increase the ways in which we normally back up what we say by showing what we mean. This is helpful in any classroom subject. We rarely rely on words alone to carry the message. So teachers, even when they are teaching in the mother tongue, *do* often say 'Do it like this' and show what is to happen rather than describing it. Or, as they tell children 'You need a sharp pencil, a ruler and a sheet of graph paper', they pick up each item in turn to emphasise and confirm the message. Teaching language lessons in the target language is very much a matter of enhancing this technique. So our 'paired reading' game can be introduced in the target language as follows by a teacher using only a limited range of vocabulary and structure.

TEACHER'S WORDS	TEACHER'S ACTIONS
(Interspersed throughout with 'Right', 'Now', 'Watch carefully, it's important'.)	*(All actions should be slightly larger than life.)*
1 Watch.	*Hold up the envelope containing the cards.*
2 Here are some cards.	*Take out the cards.*
3 Here are some picture cards . . .	*Hold up the pile of picture cards so that the children can see that there are pictures on them.*
4 and here are some sentence cards.	*Show the sentence cards in the same way.*
5 Watch carefully.	*(This tells them that it is the big moment of the demonstration!)*
6 Put the pictures like this . . .	*Show the picture cards again and put them in a pile face down. (It is worth repeating the action to stress that they are face down.)*
7 and the sentences like this.	*Deal out the sentence cards into four rows of three, face down.*
8 One . . . two . . . three . . . four . . . etc.	*(Counting as you do it usefully fills in the silence while you complete the action.)*
9 I take a card . . . Ah! It's a girl. She is wearing blue trousers and a green sweater.	*Take the top card from the picture pile, show the group and comment on it.*
10 Now I take a sentence card.	*Choose (with a touch of drama) a card from the spread of sentence cards.*
11 She is wearing red trousers.	*Hold up the sentence card (word side to the class first) then read it.*
12 Is that right? Is she wearing red trousers?	*Hold the two cards up side by side, repeating the phrase and looking from one card to the other.*

13 Trousers? . . . Yes. Red? . . .
No. It's not right.

14 So I put the picture like this . . .   *Place the picture card under the rest*
   under the others . . .   *of the pile making sure that 'under'*
                                                    is clear.

15 and I put the sentence like this   *Replace the sentence card in its*
   . . . in the same place . . .   *original position.*

and so on.

In this way, through 'demonstrating by doing' and by using sources of understanding *other than language* the teacher can explain even apparently complicated activities in very simple language. This process of teaching in English allows us to offer the children language in use not just language for exercises.

This chapter has identified three priorities:

– teaching which is based on the skills and instincts children bring with them to the classroom;
– the development of attitudes and responses which contribute to the process of developing competence in another language;
– ways of working with the language for real.

If we take these priorities seriously then we are obviously no longer talking about classrooms where the children spend all their time sitting still in rows or talking only to the teacher. We are also talking about teaching which will sometimes involve teachers in adapting the textbook or in devising activities of their own. In both respects we need to be realistic. This is the focus of the next chapter.

3

Being realistic

There are so many good language teaching ideas in circulation that it is very easy to get carried away. It is not unknown for language teachers to be found cutting up little pieces of paper, or drawing flashcards at one o'clock in the morning. It may be worthwhile. Occasionally it is absolutely necessary but basically it is not a realistic or sane way to do our job.

It is also unreasonable to imagine that all language classes take place with about fifteen children in a sound-proof room, out of sight of colleagues. Similarly, we cannot reasonably expect children to be angels. If we are encouraging them to interact, to joke, to be creative and independent, then there will be times when they become silly. There can be few teachers who can swear hand on heart that they have never heard themselves say wearily, 'O.K. If you can't be sensible about this (it's usually something really good the teacher has taken hours to prepare) we'll have to do something very boring.' For the children's sakes and ours this is a situation to avoid.

Language classrooms are potentially noisy and demanding places. We need to be realistic in our expectations of ourselves and the learners. However, this does not mean that we should cynically expect and accept the second rate. It does not mean, for example, that we should reject the idea of pairwork because our classes are big, or not very able, or poorly motivated. On the contrary, being realistic should mean taking realities into account in such a way that good things can still happen. To see how this works, let us look first at how this approach of constructive realism relates to the matter of children's behaviour in language classes.

Schools may be one of the few places left where children can find quiet and sustained application to a task in hand. How can we reconcile this need to give the children periods of sustained calm and independent work with our declared intention to promote interaction and real communication? In other words, how can we be sure that interaction and communication do not simply lead to unproductive fragmentation and restlessness? This is particularly important when our classes are large or our classrooms very cramped.

We can start by investigating two particular aspects of our lessons:

– the stir/settle factor;
– the involvement factor.

3.1
Knowing which activities 'stir' a class and which 'settle' them

You will find that some language activities stir a class. In a positive sense, 'stir' means that the activities wake them up, stimulate them. In a negative sense, it may be that the activities over-excite them or allow them to become unconstructively restless. There are other activities which have the opposite effect. They seem to settle the children. To put it positively, that means they will calm a class down. The negative side of this is to say that some activities will bore the class into inertia.

If we know the effect of activities like this, we can plan lessons which neither stay stuck in dullness nor get out of hand in excitement. So it is useful to make your own list from experience of your particular class or classes. For example, most teachers find copying quietens children like magic. So does colouring. Competitions, on the other hand, make children excited and noisy.

Another way of looking at it is in terms of the different effects of different language skills. Oral work always seems to stir. Listening usually settles. You can equally well apply the same stir/settle distinction to any typical and regular features of your teaching. For example, you perhaps have a routine oral exchange of several sentences with which you regularly begin a lesson. Ask yourself whether it basically stirs or settles. There may be occasions when it is not an appropriate start.

It will help to think of any classroom event in this way. What happens, for example, when you hand out books? If the answer in your experience is 'stir' then there will be occasions when you quite deliberately choose to delay the event until you have settled the class down. In order to have the freedom to adapt, we need to know the effect of what we do. So, either on your own or with a group of fellow teachers, you could make up a chart which reflects your experience.

For example:

Usually stirs	Usually settles
oral work	copying
competitions	colouring
lotto	listening (if they have something to do)
doing plays	
teacher + one pupil at a time	tests (if not too difficult...)
	being read to
. . . .	. . . .
. . . .	. . . .

Notice that the headings say 'usually'. This is because as soon as we start doing this, we find ourselves saying something like, 'Well oral work does stir but, in a funny sort of way, chorus work seems to calm them down'. Or 'Pairwork makes them noisy so I suppose it's a stirrer, but sometimes they get so absorbed in what they are doing that they settle'. Perhaps you find that listening to tapes settles them, but not if the recording is of a poor quality or if they can't understand anything or if they have nothing to do while they are listening. This does not invalidate the concept of stir/settle but draws our attention to another related aspect. We need to look at the involvement factor as well.

3.2
Knowing which activities engage children's minds and which keep them physically occupied

At the risk again of oversimplifying for the sake of clarity, we can identify two main types of involvement which could be described roughly as:

– mental engagement;
– actual occupation.

We can see the difference between these two forms of involvement by comparing two activities. The first is a guessing activity which can be used to provide meaningful practice of any phrases or words the children are learning. In this particular example it is intended to provide practice asking questions using 'going to' + places.

The teacher has five promptcards showing places, e.g. park, supermarket, etc.

The children are already fairly familiar with the words. They have already practised repeating the words after the teacher and are now able to produce the words by themselves if the teacher just holds up the cards without saying anything. Now comes the meaningful practice.

Guessing: To practise 'going to' + places

– The teacher gives the cards to one child who holds them so that the other children cannot see which card is at the top of the pile.
– The teacher starts the guessing:

TEACHER: Are you going to the library?
  CHILD: No.
TEACHER: Are you going to the post office?
  CHILD: No.

– The rest of the class joins in the guessing.
– When someone guesses correctly, another child chooses a card and the guessing process starts again.

In order to do this activity the children have to remember which five places are on the cards. They have to recall and produce the phrases and they have to work out by process of elimination which card their classmate must have chosen. So they have to think. The activity also engages their emotions. It is fun. They are eager to choose right. In this form then, the activity is mentally engaging in several ways. That is why children respond to it so well and why similar activities are very effective and popular.

This kind of mental and emotional engagement contrasts with actual occupation. Compare the guessing activity with what happens when we ask children to copy out a list of words. Copying is not mentally engaging. It is true that the children have to concentrate in order to copy accurately, but they do not have to think very hard. Copying is involving in a different way. It is *actually* occupying. Each child is physically doing something. It is also usually an activity where all the children in the class are *simultaneously* doing something. This contrasts with the guessing activity when only one child is speaking at a time, although we tend to think of it as a 'whole class' activity because the teacher leads it from the front.

Again it will help to make yourself a list, this time of types of work which create mental engagement and those which actually occupy the learners.

mentally engaging	actually occupying
games	reading aloud
puzzles	writing
competitions	drawing
imagining	repetition
talking about themselves	. . . .
. . . .	. . . .
. . . .	

When we identify these stir/settle or involvement elements in this way we have much more chance of avoiding a language lesson which is too rowdy or one which is too soporific. We thus have a way of making sure through positive action that the need for an interactive classroom does not automatically lead to restless and silly behaviour, even when the classes are big. For example, the teacher can now do two things:

– choose a style of work that in terms of its stir/settle potential suits a particular class or occasion;
– increase children's involvement by adapting activities so that, if possible, they offer both mental engagement and actual occupation, preferably of the whole class at the same time.

3.3 Choosing the style to suit the mood

There will be occasions when your class comes to the language lesson on a 'high'. Sometimes it is because they have just had sport or a lunch break. Sometimes they have been with another teacher who keeps them silent nearly all the time, or one who has little control over them. In either case, the effect will be the same. They will arrive at the language lesson in a state of noise and energy. Or maybe you are their class teacher so they have been with you all the time. Even so, there are occasions when they will start the English lesson unsettled. You may have just been discussing a future school outing about which they have got excited. You may have been asked by the head teacher to make a special announcement that next Monday will be fancy dress day in school to raise money for charity. Perhaps you have made the class stop working on something they were enjoying but which you want to continue tomorrow. Alternatively, it may just be the weather, or a wasp, or the window cleaner, or the class clown on particularly good form. The list is endless. When these kinds of things happen, it is instinctive to calm the children down in some way. However, recent language teaching has tended to follow patterns of work which do not help to calm the children but instead stir them up! For example, we are often encouraged to start lessons with a ritual oral exchange or an oral recap of the previous day's work. Next, there is often an oral introduction of new vocabulary. This is probably followed by oral practice of various kinds. All this may take up the first twenty minutes or more of the lesson. In fact, it is not uncommon to see lessons which are entirely oral. It is certainly possible to teach like this but there is a danger. In the kind of lesson pattern just described, there is a strong chance that only the will power and strong presence of the teacher prevents the class from becoming rather silly, because all these are stirring activities. If they are also low on actual occupation (e.g. if most of them only involve one child at a time) and also offer little compensatory mental engagement (e.g. if they provide a lot of plain repetition rather than real use) then the risk of unwelcome and inappropriate behaviour is even greater.

There is clearly no point in letting matters get out of hand or engaging in a battle of wills with the class just because we are 'supposed' to structure lessons in this way. Stick to your instincts as a teacher. So, you might want to think of a brief 'settler' to start off with, even if it isn't what you would have chosen to do under other circumstances. For example, it can help with a difficult or restless class to start a lesson with something settling and actively occupying like copying out a short list of words which the children are going to use later. (If you don't want the children's pronunciation to be distorted by having the written word in front of them when you come to the oral work, you can always clean the board and get them to close their exercise books so they can no longer see what they have written until they are ready for it.) For a class that cannot write, you can still do a pencil and paper settler. Here is an example.

A 'settling' version of revision of the previous lesson's vocabulary

– Stick five flashcards on the
   board and number them.

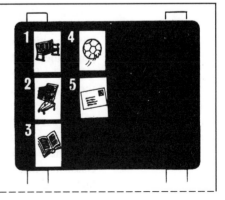

   – Say the phrases or words represented by the cards and the class writes
      the numbers in the order you say them, e.g. in the above example, the
      teacher says:

      'I am going to the supermarket.'
      'I am going to the sports centre.'
      'I am going to the library.'

      and the children write down the numbers 2 4 3.
   – Do this several times in a row with the same phrases or words, just
      varying the order.

This is not a mindless repressive activity. It gives the class the chance to hear the words over and over again and they have to recognise the meaning of what you are saying in order to choose the correct picture. But at the same time it keeps them occupied and settled.

We can adjust the middle of the lesson too to fit the class mood. If the middle of the lesson is getting a bit too restless, most of us instinctively change activities. But if the class is getting silly we need to make sure we change to something settling. So look for settling versions of what you want to do. For example, perhaps you plan some fun listening practice in the form of lotto but when it gets to that point of the lesson the class are silly or just generally restless. So, instead of lotto, which is stirring, you could use the 'write down the number of the one I'm saying' activity which has just been described. It involves exactly the same language and learning processes as lotto but does so calmly. This activity works equally well as a settler anywhere in the lesson.

There will be other occasions when you will want to achieve the reverse and wake the class up a little at the beginning of the lesson or part way through when interest is flagging. Again you can choose an activity which encourages that, even if under other circumstances you might have done it differently or at another point in the lesson. This last point needs to be stressed. There are certain conventions about language teaching which seem to imply that some things are 'good' in absolute terms and other things are 'bad'. Teachers can sometimes be made to feel very guilty about setting the children to copy, for example, or about letting them write the words before they hear them. The truth is that however potentially valuable these conventions are as guidelines, they *are* only guidelines. No activity or particular sequence of activities is good if it is in the wrong place in terms of the human reactions to the lesson. If you have the kind of class that can cope with twenty to thirty minutes of teacher/pupil one-at-a-time oral work, then you may want to teach like that though it remains a fairly inefficient use of any single child's time and is exhausting for the teacher. But many classes will not maintain interest for that long if they are not settled or involved. When that happens in your classroom, then the activity *on this occasion* is no good whatever its theoretical potential. Flowers are weeds when there are too many of them or they are in the wrong place!

There is something else a teacher can do to improve the quality of classroom interaction on the basis of the insights afforded by the stir/settle factor and the involvement factor. You can look for ways to *combine* mental engagement and actual occupation. This is a strategy which is particularly helpful with large classes.

Take, for example, a mentally engaging activity like the one just described where the children are trying to guess which picture or word one of their classmates has chosen. This will keep even a large class happy for a while because it is fun and it makes them think. Even so, there are two disadvantages. First, any single child in the class is not likely to have more than one or possibly two opportunities to speak. Secondly, only one child is speaking at any given time. However, once you have established how the guessing works you can then change the activity into simultaneous pairwork for the whole class, adding actual occupation to the mental engagement of the original idea.

Guessing: Pairwork activity to continue practising 'going to' + places

The children work in pairs so that all the class is working at the same time.

Materials: The five promptcards to represent the places.

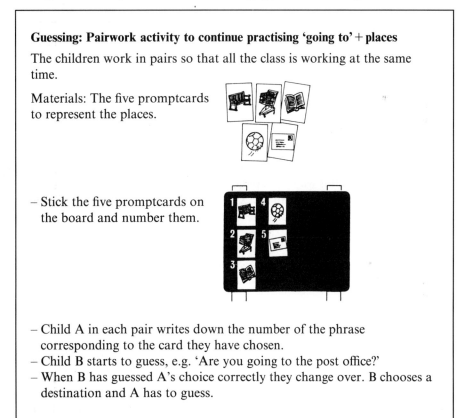

– Stick the five promptcards on the board and number them.

– Child A in each pair writes down the number of the phrase corresponding to the card they have chosen.
– Child B starts to guess, e.g. 'Are you going to the post office?'
– When B has guessed A's choice correctly they change over. B chooses a destination and A has to guess.

In the same way, you can increase the mental engagement element of an activity which is physically occupying but otherwise fairly mindless. For example, suppose you want to help children to make a list in their books of some of the words they have been using. They can, of course, just copy out the list from the board. There will be times when that is all you want them to do. But there will be other times when you will want to help them get the words firmly into their heads as well as into their books. Writing the word just once does not provide much practice and it is possible to copy out words and phrases without thinking very much about what they mean. One way to increase the mental engagement and thereby to increase the chances of effective learning is to ask the children to list words in categories. Here is an example.

Categorising activity to practise words for the topic of shopping

Stage 1: Getting the children to think of the words for themselves

– On the board write the names of about five shops. (It helps to include supermarket for reasons that will become obvious!)
– Individually or in pairs, the children start making a list of things they could buy in these shops. At this stage, it makes sense to use rough paper as they are writing down half remembered spellings. It doesn't matter if their spelling is inventive or their memory of the words is imprecise. What matters is that *they* think of the words not you.

Stage 2: Checking the spelling

– Ask the children for the words they have thought of and write these up on another part of the board. In this way you are now providing a correct version so they can check their spelling.

Stage 3: Showing them how to categorise

– Start allocating the items to the appropriate headings on the board. You can get the children to help you:

TEACHER: Where can I buy bread?
CHILD A: Baker.
TEACHER: Yes, at the baker's.
    (Writes it under the correct heading.)
    Where else?
CHILD B: At the supermarket.

and so on.
– Do a couple of examples like this and then set the children to write the category headings in their books and to copy the items into any column they think is appropriate.

In this way, you have retained the actual occupation of copying but you have added to it the mental engagement of thinking. (There are some slightly more fun versions of this activity on page 97.)

Any teacher reading this is probably beginning to think, 'This is all very well, but when am I supposed to find the time and energy to work this all out in my lesson planning?' This brings us back to the second area where constructive realism is needed. Primary language teaching seems to make very considerable and often unreasonable demands on a teacher's preparation time. It does, of course, help to get the children to make some of the actual materials for you. They can cut things up or colour things in, for example. We can also take comfort in the fact that some of the most effective ideas in the classroom are very simple and easy to set up, like the 'guess which one I've chosen' activity mentioned earlier.

There are also three other main ways we can help ourselves. We need to remember to:

– keep the lesson simple;
– reuse materials;
– reuse ideas.

3.4
Keeping the lesson simple

We are often told that we should make our lessons varied. This is good advice but it is also open to misunderstanding. Variation can be interpreted in two different ways with very different effects.

You can make a lesson varied by doing lots of activities on different topics. If that is what we mean by variation then we may produce a lesson which, say, begins with five minutes of greetings, then revises numbers, does a quick introduction of colours and finishes off by singing a song about the days of the week. This is patently not a helpful form of variation. The children's minds are being required to jump from one topic to the next with little time to let things sink in or rehearse things effectively through meaningful use. So what has gone wrong? The answer is probably that the teacher is trying to compensate for the fact that many of our learners seem to have a horribly short concentration span. Sometimes, too, the problem is that the teacher feels that the fact that the children cannot yet write much in English means that the whole lesson should be oral work, and therefore feels that the only way to introduce variety is to alter the topic of the oral work. There are three things to note here.

– We won't help the children to develop their capacity to concentrate if we jump inconsequentially from one topic to the next.
– There are ways of varying the oral work so that it is making different demands on the children and therefore *feels different* even when the topic remains the same.
– Even if a group of children cannot write English or if your syllabus suggests they should not write English in the early stages, there are other kinds of pencil and paper work they can do.

So, variation does not mean we have to keep changing the topic. Instead, we can keep to the same topic and materials and change the work we do. If, at the same time, we keep an eye on the stir/settle and involvement factors, then it is perfectly possible to devise a varied lesson on as little as five words for as long as an hour. You are not very likely to want to do this but it makes the point. So, here is an example of an hour's varied lesson for beginners. It is based on just five colours and the activities it uses are each very unpretentious but together make for a satisfying lesson. (Please note that this and any other activity written out in detail in this book is not intended as an example of how it *should* be done but how it *could* be done.)

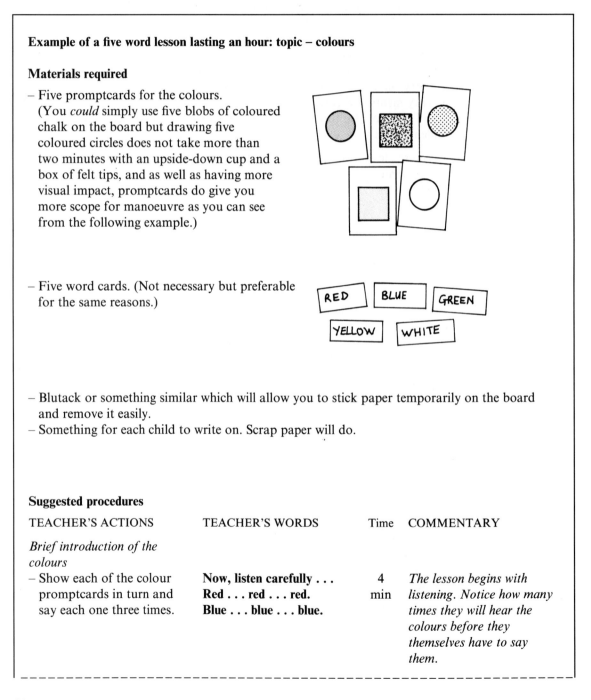

Example of a five word lesson lasting an hour: topic – colours

Materials required

– Five promptcards for the colours. (You *could* simply use five blobs of coloured chalk on the board but drawing five coloured circles does not take more than two minutes with an upside-down cup and a box of felt tips, and as well as having more visual impact, promptcards do give you more scope for manoeuvre as you can see from the following example.)

– Five word cards. (Not necessary but preferable for the same reasons.)

– Blutack or something similar which will allow you to stick paper temporarily on the board and remove it easily.
– Something for each child to write on. Scrap paper will do.

Suggested procedures

TEACHER'S ACTIONS	TEACHER'S WORDS	Time	COMMENTARY
Brief introduction of the colours			
– Show each of the colour promptcards in turn and say each one three times.	**Now, listen carefully . . .** **Red . . . red . . . red.** **Blue . . . blue . . . blue.**	4 min	*The lesson begins with listening. Notice how many times they will hear the colours before they themselves have to say them.*

TEACHER'S ACTIONS	TEACHER'S WORDS	Time	COMMENTARY

– Stick each colour card on the board. Say the colours once or twice again as you do so.

Listen again . . .
Red . . . red.
Blue . . . blue.
Green . . . green. etc.

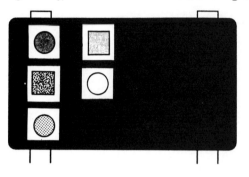

– Get a child to come to the front and to point to the colours you say. Do this several times with four or five different children.

Anna, come here. . . . Red?
(Child points.)
Yes . . . red! Green?
(Child points.)
Yes . . . green! etc.

It is best not to take too long over this introduction. It is not very involving and is therefore potentially a 'stir' activity.

Activity 1: 'Write down the number of the one I say'

– Write a number alongside each of the colours.

NOW, watch carefully.
1, 2, 3, 4, 5.

9 min

Words like NOW, OK, RIGHT, etc. help to emphasise stages and give a feeling of progress even though the activities are quite similar.

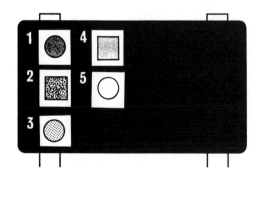

TEACHER'S ACTIONS	TEACHER'S WORDS	Time	COMMENTARY
– Say one of the colours and on another part of the board write down its number. Do this for all five colours but in any order you like.	**Blue . . . 2 (writes).** **Yellow . . . 4 (writes).** **Red . . . 1 (writes). etc.**		

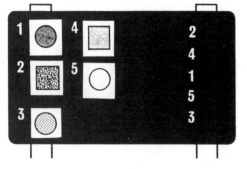

– Do the same again but get one of the children to write up on the board the number of the colours you say.			
– Do it again but this time get the whole class to write down the numbers (rough paper is best).			*Settler needed so change to simultaneous involvement.*
– Do this several times. Check after each turn by writing the sequence of numbers up quickly on the board. The children can then quickly check their own answers.	**Let's check.** **Red . . . 1. Blue . . . 2.** **White . . . 5. etc.** **Who got three right?** **Two? Four? Five?**		

Activity 2: True/false

– Say a number and say a colour. The children have to decide whether they belong together.	**T: NOW, listen carefully.** **White . . . 3. Is that true?** **Child 1: No.** **(Teacher writes N for 'No' on board.)** **T: Green . . . 3. Is that true?** **Child 2: Yes.** **(Teacher writes Y for 'Yes' on the board.)**	5 min	*Time for some mental engagement.*
– Do this orally first, then turn it into a pencil and paper activity. The children write Y for 'Yes' and N for 'No' on their piece of rough paper.			*Now add simultaneous actual involvement.*

TEACHER'S ACTIONS	TEACHER'S WORDS	Time	COMMENTARY

Activity 3: Memory true/false

– This is basically the same as the previous activity but this time get the children to close their eyes so they have to *remember* what was on the board.

– To make this more challenging you can change the cards around to different numbers. Give the class 3 seconds to remember which card is at which number. When they get too good at that arrangement, change the cards around again.

NOW, look carefully. (As before in Activity 2.)

5 min

The fun element increases the mental engagement.

Activity 4: Energetic true/false

– The same basic activity but this time they stand up if it's true and sit down if it's false. Try to catch them out by doing it at speed.

**NOW, watch . . .
If it's true, STAND UP (teacher stands).
If it's false, SIT DOWN (teacher sits).
So . . . Green . . . 3 (stands up).**

3 min

Increased fun element. This is a stirring activity but it has been preceded by settlers so it should not be a problem.

Activity 5: Repetition

– Do plenty of straightforward repetition both in chorus and individually. Check pronunciation carefully.

**Well done . . .
NOW . . .**

3 min

Now, only now, we come to speaking activities. We need to resettle the class here. Oral work is noisy but chorus work is involving. This is also the time for accuracy practice.

TEACHER'S ACTIONS	TEACHER'S WORDS	Time	COMMENTARY

Activity 6: Disappearing cards

– Get the class to say (in chorus) the colours in sequence.	**Good . . . NOW . . . look carefully.** **Red, blue, green, yellow, white.** **Say it with me . . .** **red, blue, green, yellow, white.** **NOW!** **(Just point.)**	5 min	*Increase their mental engagement in the speaking by challenging their memory.*

– Remove one of the cards from
  somewhere in the sequence.

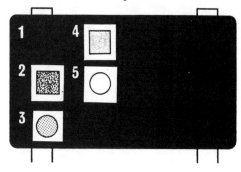

– The class now choruses
  the *whole* sequence
  including the missing
  card. (It helps them if
  you touch the board for
  each colour, including
  the empty space.)
– Remove another card
  and get the children to
  say the whole sequence
  again.
– Continue until there are
  no cards on the board
  and the children are
  saying the whole
  sequence from memory!
– Let two or three children
  say it solo.
– You can change the
  sequence and repeat the
  activity.

*Once the class is familiar
with this activity, add to the
involvement by getting
another child to be teacher.*

TEACHER'S ACTIONS	TEACHER'S WORDS	Time	COMMENTARY
Activity 7: 'Guess what'			
– Choose one of the cards and write its number somewhere on the board but conceal it so the children cannot see what you have chosen.	**That was good!** **NOW, watch.**	8 min	*More mentally engaging speaking. This is also a time for fluency.*
– Get the children to guess which colour you have chosen.	**Guess! . . . Is it red? Blue?** **White?** **Child 1: Yellow.** **T: No!** **Child 2: Red.** **T: No!** **etc.**		
– After you have had several turns and have established what is happening, call a child to the front to choose a card secretly in the same way.			
– Continue with this, giving plenty of children the chance to participate.			
Activity 8: Paired 'guess what'			
– This is the same activity but done in simultaneous pairs. Child A writes down the number of a card. Child B guesses the colour.	**NOW, in twos (pointing) 1,** **2 . . . 1, 2 . . . with a** **partner.**	5 min	*Need to increase actual occupation again so this activity provides simultaneous involvement.*

TEACHER'S ACTIONS	TEACHER'S WORDS	Time	COMMENTARY

Activity 9: Recognition reading

– Stick up your word cards in jumbled sequence on the other side of the board, saying them as you do so.	OK. . . . **Look.** **(Reading) yellow, white, red, etc.** **OK. NOW, watch.**	5 min	*Back to teacher control in order to settle things down again after pairwork.*

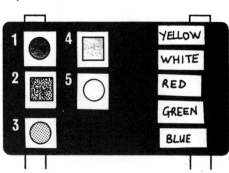

– Read one of the word cards. 'Search' for the matching colour card and move the word card over to stick it alongside.	**Blue . . . er . . . blue . . .** **(Picks word card and moves it across.)** **. . . blue.** **Yellow . . . er . . . yellow.** **etc.**		

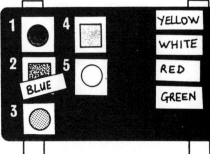

– Repeat the process several times over to establish the pattern. – Move the word cards back to the far side of the board. – Call a child to come to the front. You read the card. The child has to identify the written card for the colour you are saying and then move it over to the correct colour card. Repeat this plenty of different times with different children.	**Thomas, come here. . . .** **Yellow!** **(Child picks a word card and moves it across.)** **Yes, well done!** **NOW, green . . . etc.**		*Searching for the right card provides some mental engagement for the whole class as they watch but it offers little actual involvement for most children so . . .*

TEACHER'S ACTIONS	TEACHER'S WORDS	Time	COMMENTARY

Activity 10: Reading aloud

– Leave the colour cards and word cards matched up alongside each other and get the class to 'read' the words, repeating after you and then reading without you while you just point. Start with chorus work, then ask individual children and switch back to chorus work if the rest look like falling asleep!

3 min

Change to simultaneous involvement.

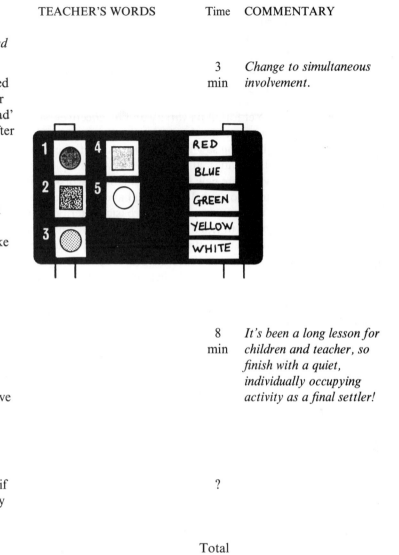

Activity 11: Writing

– The class copies up the list of words and then draws in the colours. (Useful rule: no colouring until they have been checked as accurate!)

8 min

It's been a long lesson for children and teacher, so finish with a quiet, individually occupying activity as a final settler!

Activity 12: Standby

– In the remaining time, if any, you can repeat any one of the previous activities.

?

Total = 60 min

For all its repetition of the same five words, the children will not find this lesson either unduly repetitive or boring. Notice that the variation comes in the forms of activity. Meanwhile, the focus is comfortingly clear and secure. The children can feel their competence being built up as they tackle each new aspect of the work. They hear plenty before they speak, so that when they speak it comes out confidently and already fairly accurately. Reading and writing are built on the other skills so they confirm rather than confuse. There is mental engagement as well as actual involvement and the actual involvement is made simultaneous as often as possible. In this way, however big the class, any one child has plenty to do in the lesson and plenty of language practice. The pace of the lesson is also managed so as to provide a shift from settling activity to stirring and back to settling. In this way, the teacher can quietly keep everything under control without that control having to be explicit. This improves the general atmosphere of the classroom. There is scope too for conscious focus on accuracy and correction as well as time for fun and real language use. There are times for work with the teacher, times with friends and times to work quietly alone.

Yet for all its variety and its effectiveness the lesson is not complicated. Written out like this in detail it inevitably looks far more complicated than it would if you saw it in practice. In fact, the lesson is built up of a sequence of small activities, all of which are very simple and straightforward. (If the activities are new to you, it might be worth trying them out separately first to get used to them.) Once you have tried a lesson like this several times, you will find that you can use it as a basic pattern of work for almost any set of items you want to teach. It is particularly useful as a basic format where you are having to teach without a coursebook. It also shows how one modest set of materials, in this case the coloured cards, can be used for many different activities. There are other ways in which we can reuse materials.

3.5 Reusing materials

We have just seen how one set of promptcards can be used to provide a whole lesson of different activities around the same topic. Other materials are also reusable round the same theme. For example, if you go to the trouble of drawing a set of grids for an activity or take up time in a lesson getting the children to draw one, you don't want to use it for two minutes and then move on to something else. So this single grid:

could be used and reused in the following ways.

– Listening activity. The children listen to a series of statements made by the teacher and then fill in the appropriate reference point on the matrix:
'Claudia likes apples and bananas.'

– Speaking activities based on true/false. Once the grid has been filled in the teacher could use it to ask true/false questions:
'Claudia likes grapes. True or false?'

– Simultaneous pairwork:

Paolo likes bananas and grapes

Yes he does

– Writing. The children use the information on their grid to make up sentences and write them down:

Luisa likes apples and grapes.

You could spread these activities out over more than one lesson or use them in various combinations in one lesson. Either way, by this time the grids will have amply repaid the initial time taken up in drawing them.

Remember too that particular promptcards or even grids can act as prompts for a wide range of different phrases and exchanges provided we make it clear what we are doing.

For example, on different occasions, the card above could be the prompt for several very different language exchanges, e.g.:

'Have you got a bike?' 'Your bike is great.'
'Can I borrow your bike?' 'How much does a bike cost?'
'I like cycling!' 'Please can I have a bike?'
'Let's go for a bike ride.' 'Where is my bike?'
and so on. . . .

If you are going to reuse promptcards in this way then you will want to keep them very simple. They are probably best drawn in black, thickish lines giving an essential outline and without any writing. This is because writing tends to tie the card down to representing just one phrase.

Finally, as well as looking for different ways in which we can use one set of materials and thus reduce our preparation load, we can also reduce our *thinking* preparation. It is possible to do this by identifying a core of activity types which we can use and reuse in order to teach different language content.

3.6
Reusing a core of ideas

It has already been suggested that the 'guess which one I have chosen' activity set out earlier in this chapter could be used to practise almost any phrase. It is only a matter of working out the appropriate guessing question. The 'write down the number of the one you hear' activity on page 41 transfers equally easily to any set of language items or structures you wish to practise. Or the basic grid format can be used for any two elements you wish to combine, for example, people and what they like eating, days of the week and the weather.

There are more examples in the practical activities section at the end of this chapter. The point is that because these activities are simple in principle, they will transfer to all kinds of topics and situations. Because you use them regularly you will quickly get to know the best way to set them up with your classes. Because the classes know them, they will take to them easily when they appear. You will also, through using these activities often, get to know which of them are good as stirrers and which act as settlers. You will develop ways of adapting them to actual as well as mental involvement. They can become truly the core of your language teaching.

In *Practical Activities 1* which follows, certain activities have been marked as the kind of activities that can easily form an effective core. They are, however, very much a personal choice, offered as a starting point not a prescription. Choose your own core activities as soon as you can.

> This chapter has suggested ways of applying what it calls constructive realism to questions of classroom behaviour and preparation load. The considerations of stir/settle, the concepts of mental engagement and actual occupation, and the comments about variation and simplicity will help you to evaluate the activities offered in the next section.

Practical Activities 1

Introduction

This section of the book offers a collection of practical ideas for the classroom based on the preceding chapters. The activities suggested are based very firmly on the priorities identified in Chapter 2. They are all intended to encourage real language exchanges and to develop confidence and willingness to have a go. They are also designed to build on the capacities (discussed in Chapter 1) which the children bring to the lesson. So the activities exploit and develop the capacity for interaction and talk, the capacity for indirect learning, the capacity for creative use of language resources, and the capacity for play and fun. While you read them, it will also be helpful to consider their potential role as 'stirrers' or 'settlers' and to think about whether they offer actual or mental involvement along the lines discussed in Chapter 3.

The activities are grouped according to the nature of the response they demand from the children and the nature of the experience they offer them. It would have been possible to categorise activities in terms of the language skill being developed (e.g. listening), or the topics (e.g. the family), or the 'mode' of working (e.g. pairwork). However, the present headings were chosen in the belief that when sharing ideas with other teachers, the actual format or linguistic content of the activity is less important than the kind of experience it offers the children and the principles on which it is based. This is because precise formats do not necessarily transfer very easily from one set of circumstances to another. Something which works in one teacher's classroom may not work in another's in exactly the same way. On the other hand, if the underlying principle of an activity is clear, then each of us can give it a form which suits our circumstances.

The activities can be used occasionally to supplement a textbook or they can stand on their own as the basis for an independent programme. Most of the activities can be used in either simpler or more complex forms and are therefore suitable for any age group. The few exceptions to this are indicated.

Some of the activities are marked with ****. This does not mean that they are necessarily the best! It means that they are a personal choice of activities suitable for the kind of 'core' repertoire which has just been discussed in Chapter 3.

Finally, to repeat a point made earlier, the detailed procedures are intended as an example of how you *could* do the activity not how you *must* do it.

GROUP **1**

'Do something about it!'

The particular intention behind this first group of activities is to strengthen understanding by linking it to active response. For example, it is usually important when organising listening activities to make sure that the children have something to do as a result of what they hear. This means that they are having to process the language they hear, and are not just letting the noise of it into their ears.

Activity **1**
Write down the number of the one you hear ****

In this activity the children have to identify which promptcard you are talking about. This is a very simple activity and as the four stars show, is one you might consider making part of your core. It is useful as a way of introducing something new. It is a way of providing plenty of meaningful listening practice before the children are asked to produce the sounds themselves. There was an example of this in the five word lesson on page 28. There, it was being used to introduce colours. In this example, it is being used for a different purpose but the process is the same.

Language focus in this example

Understanding directions, e.g. turn left, turn right, go straight on, cross the bridge, take the second right, take the third left.

Materials required

– A set of drawings to prompt the language you want to practise, e.g.:

NOTE 1: You can simply draw the symbols on the board or make a quick set of promptcards. Promptcards take time to make initially but have the advantage that you can move them around. You can hold them, arrange them in various combinations on the board, or hand them out to pupils. They do not have to be complicated. Some of the commercial flashcards are very attractive but too detailed, big and heavy. If you make your own cards, you do not have to go to the expense of buying actual card. You can use paper. One sheet of ordinary A4 paper will make four 'cards' of about the right size. Use a strong coloured and thickish felt tip pen and just draw the essential elements or a symbol rather than a detailed picture. Children are quite happy with this. It is also easier for you.

NOTE 2: You don't have to have promptcards to do this activity. In fact, in most of the activities suggesting cards, you can write or draw on the board instead, though it is slower and more restricting.

– Blutack or something similar which can be used to stick the cards temporarily to the board.
– The children need something to write on. Rough paper will do.

Preliminary work

Briefly introduce the new phrases in the following way.

– Stick each prompt on the board, saying each one once or twice again as you do so:

TEACHER: Turn right . . . turn right . . . turn right. . . .

– Stick each prompt on the board, saying each one once or twice again as you do so:

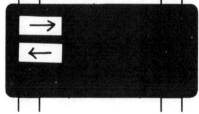

TEACHER: Turn right . . . turn right. . . .
             Turn left . . . turn left. . . .

– Go through the whole set of promptcards once more fairly quickly.
– Get a child to come to the front and point to whichever one you say. Do this several times with different children.

Now move on to 'write down the number of the one you hear'.

Suggested procedures

– Number the
  prompts on
  the board.

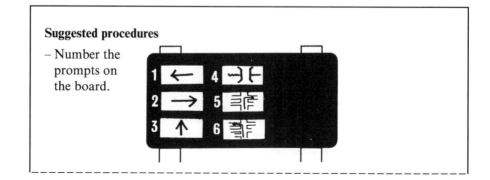

– Say one of the phrases and, on another part of the board, write its number. Do this for all the phrases but in any order you like.

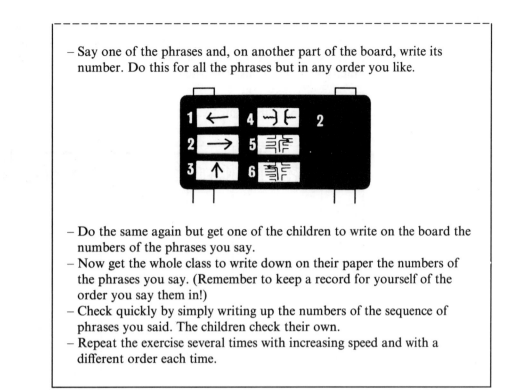

– Do the same again but get one of the children to write on the board the numbers of the phrases you say.
– Now get the whole class to write down on their paper the numbers of the phrases you say. (Remember to keep a record for yourself of the order you say them in!)
– Check quickly by simply writing up the numbers of the sequence of phrases you said. The children check their own.
– Repeat the exercise several times with increasing speed and with a different order each time.

Variation

To practise parts of the body you can get the children to draw a pin man and to write the numbers on the appropriate parts.

Other language you can practise with this activity

This is one of those activities you can use to introduce any group of words or phrases you want to teach.

Final comments

This is an example of an exercise which provides 'written' work without expecting the children to be able to write. Because it is a listening activity and because it occupies the whole class at the same time, it makes a good settler to start a lesson with and can also be used mid-lesson to calm a class down.

Activity **2**
Listening grid
****

Here is another activity suitable for your 'core'. It too is intended to provide active response to new language. For this activity, the children have to mark on a matrix or grid the information read out by the teacher. The example below is practising prepositions. The teacher has so far read out:

'The cup is on the table.'
'The cat is under the chair.'
'The girl is in front of the tree.'

Language focus in this example

Describing where things are.

Materials required

– A small grid for each child.

NOTE: If it makes life easier for you, there is no reason why they should not draw their own grids, but it takes time so if you are fortunate enough to have access to a photocopier, it is much simpler to draw the grids and duplicate them yourself. They do not have to be big. Dividing an A4-sized piece of paper into four is perfectly satisfactory. It also cuts down on costs!

– Promptcards which are the same as the pictures on the grid.
– Blutack or something similar which will allow you to stick your pictures temporarily on the board.

Preliminary work

The previous 'write down the number' activity makes a very good lead-in to this.

Suggested procedures

– First pre-check the various elements of the grid quickly and build up an example grid on the board. You can do this by saying each phrase two or three times and putting the matching promptcard up as you say it, in the same position as it appears in the grid:

TEACHER: On the chair . . . on the chair.
Behind the tree . . . behind the tree.
Under the table . . . under the table.

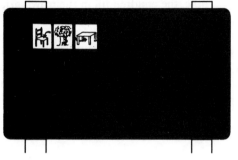

In this way, build up the complete grid pattern of cards on the board.

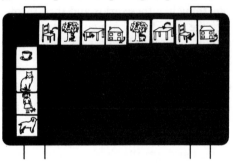

(If the class look as if they are falling asleep, you can slip in the occasional chorus repetition, but at this stage you are still just asking them to listen.)

– Now draw in the lines round your cards so you have a board grid.
– Make a statement and mark in the appropriate box:

TEACHER: The cat is on the table.

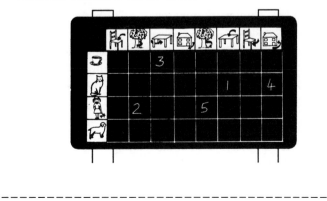

- Do several examples like this yourself then get a child to come to the board to write the numbers in the appropriate squares. (With some classes you may want to do this several times to check their understanding before you start them working on their own.)
- Hand out the class grids.
- Rub out the numbers from the grid on the board and start again. This time, the children fill in their own grids. If some of the class are looking a little unsure, you can always do the first one or two on your board grid with them so they can see that they have got the right idea.
- When you have finished, check by reading through the statements again and getting a child or children to write up the numbers on the board grid. Each of the class checks their own grid against the board version as you go through it.

Possible follow up

As Chapter 3 pointed out, you do not want to spend a long time preparing something like these grids and then throw them away after five minutes. So, once the grids have been completed as a listening exercise, you can use them again in several different ways, either immediately or in a later lesson. For example:

a) Further listening: True/false

- Make a statement like '2 . . . The cat is on the chair.'
- The class look at the grid and tell you 'Yes, it is.' or 'No, it isn't.'
- When you have done this several times, you can rub off the answers from the board grid, get the children to turn their grids over, and challenge them to say from memory whether your statement is true or false.

b) Later oral work with the teacher

At a later stage, after the children have done some repetition work of the phrases and can now say them well, you can go back to the grids and the class can challenge you and each other to a game of true/false along the lines described above.

c) Later oral work in pairs

Once they can say the phrases and are used to playing true/false with you as a class, they can do the activity in pairs. Child A looks at the grid to 'memorise' it, then turns it over so she can't see it. Child B then makes a statement from his grid, e.g. 'The dog is behind the tree.' Child A has to say 'Yes, it is./No, it isn't.'

d) Later written work

After they have done some reading work on the phrases, you can get them to make up and write out several sentences of their own from the grid.

| Variation | These grids are simplest if you have only one piece of information per line and if you give the information in the order it appears on the grid, so that the children do not have to search too frantically. On the other hand, more able or older children will enjoy having to search all over the grid for what you have just said. By altering the order in which you give the information you can adjust the level of the activity to suit your class. |

Other language you can practise with this activity

The possibilities are almost limitless but, for example, you could combine:

Colours and clothes.	Places and directions for getting to them.
Times and activities.	People and activities.
People and places.	Days of the week and the weather.
Rooms and furniture.	Shops and things bought in them.
	etc.

Final comments

This kind of listening grid has a great deal to commend it. It involves all the children in the class at the same time. It makes them think hard about what they are hearing and is therefore mentally engaging as well as actually occupying. It can provide worthwhile sustained listening work so we don't rush too soon into oral work with new language. It is a 'writing' activity they can do long before they can write the words. It is also possible for all children in a mixed ability class to work with the same grid quite happily. That is why it is recommended as a core activity.

Activity **3**
Listen and find

This is a rather more lively activity. This time the children have to pick out the real object which the teacher is talking about. In the example here it is a team game. In fact it is quite a 'stirrer'. It is designed to provide physically active listening practice *before* the children have moved on to speaking. (It can of course also be used later as a fun revision activity too.) The version described here is called 'The washing line game'.

Language focus in this example

Clothes and colours.

Materials required

– At the front of the room, have two boxes or bags, each containing identical sets of the items you want to practise.
– Some clothes pegs if you have them, but they are not essential.

Preliminary work

Pre-check the vocabulary in some way, even if they seemed to know it yesterday! You can do this by just telling them quickly, or by doing a 'write down the number' activity of the kind we have just looked at on page 41.

Suggested procedures

– At the front of the class, get two children to hold a short length of rope between them like a washing line.

– Divide the class into two teams and get a representative of each team to come to the front.
– Ask for an item from one of the boxes:

TEACHER: Please bring me a blue sock.

– The two representatives search their boxes to identify and take out the object concerned. The first one to hang it on the line is the winner and that team scores a point.

Variation

If your classes come to school reasonably well provided with felt tip pens or crayons and if they like drawing, you could practise the same items in the form of a kind of drawn lotto. It would look like this:

Suggested procedures

– Each child draws their own small washing line with four items of clothing on it. They then put a dot of colour on it to show what colour it is. (If we let them colour them in properly, it will be next week before some of them have finished!)
– You read out a list of items:

'I have a blue sock.'
'I also have a green shirt.'
'I have a red shirt . . .
and a blue skirt . . .'

and so on until one child has been able to cross off all the items on their line and has won that round. Remember to keep a list of what you say or you will have a rebellion on your hands!

Other language you can practise with this activity	This activity is more suited to practising separate vocabulary items rather than whole phrases. It is most fun if you can use real objects but it is perfectly possible to do it with two sets of picture cards or word cards.
Final comment	Any competition like this tends to stir a class up so you will probably want to follow it with something settling.

Activity 4
Listen and arrange

This time the children are being asked to arrange a picture or diagram according to the information they hear. This is another activity which aims to strengthen understanding by linking it to response. It again asks the children to respond physically to what they hear, although not in the energetic way that the washing line game demands. It is not such obvious fun as the washing line game but is still mentally engaging because the children have to work out the significance of what they hear. At the same time, it is much more involving than the washing line game because every child is doing something at each moment. That makes it a good settler.

Language focus in this example: Rooms in the house.

Materials required
– For this activity you need, for each child or pair of children, a base sheet like this one of the house and some name slips. If the children in your class are used to using scissors, they can cut out the name slips for you and put them in an envelope at the end of the activity. You can then reuse the materials with another class or on another occasion.
– Blutack if you have it.

49

Preliminary work

To show the class what to do, you need five names on slips of paper and an outline of the house on the board.

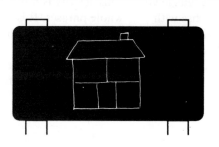

– Make a statement like: 'Lizzie is in the bedroom.' and stick the name slip in the appropriate place.

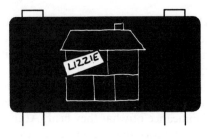

NOTE: It is better to stick the name slip in the right place if you can, because that is what the children are going to have to do. Otherwise, you can simply write in the names on the board.

– Do a couple more examples with them, glancing round to see if most of the children are following.
– Remove the name slips.

The children should now be ready to work on their own.

Suggested procedures

– Hand out the base sheets to the class. If you have not already done so, the children write the five names on the name slips and cut them out.
– Make the first statement, e.g. 'Kevin is in the bedroom.'
– The children put the name slip in the right room. (You can check supportively for the first one or two by putting the names in the right place on the board after they have all had the chance to put theirs on their sheets. In this way, you and the class will know that all is well.)
– Continue until all the name slips are placed.
– Use your board version to check back.
– Repeat the exercise as often as you like, changing the combinations of people and rooms.

Possible follow up   You can follow up with the same activities as were suggested for following up the listening grid (page 46).

Variation   This activity can also be changed to an interactive activity for pairs like the arrange and describe activity on page 14.

Other language you can practise with this activity   This activity lends itself best to any work involving locations, for example:

Shops in a street.

Furniture in a room.

Or, by using speech bubbles, you could also use it for phrases and expressions:

Final comment   The advantage of this paper arranging activity is that you can reuse your base sheet because the children are not writing on it. You can also reuse the same base sheet on another occasion but with different items to arrange.

Activity **5**
Listen and work out the order   In this activity, the children are given a set of pictures which are in the wrong order. The teacher describes the pictures in the correct order and the children have to identify them in sequence. They may not understand everything they hear. That is quite deliberate. We are encouraging them to use their ability to work on partial information and to take risks. It is easier for them to do both these things with listening than speaking, because they are being asked to respond not to produce the language themselves.

Language focus in this example   Food.

Materials required   – For each child or pair of children you need a sheet of pictures like the example below. (Remember they are in the wrong order!)

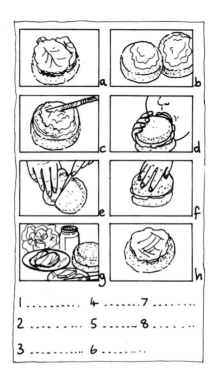

– For yourself you need a list of sentences which describe the pictures. These are in the *right* order:

To make a ham and lettuce sandwich

1. You need a slice of ham, a roll, some lettuce, some butter and some mayonnaise.
2. First cut the roll in half.
3. Butter the two pieces of roll.
4. Put the ham onto the bottom half of the roll.
5. Spread a little mayonnaise onto the ham. Be careful! Not too much!
6. Now put some lettuce on top of the ham.
7. Put the top of the roll on top and press it down.
8. Eat it!

Preliminary work

This activity would fit well into the general topic of food. It is best if the children already know the words for some of the food which comes into the activity, but it is not necessary for them to know everything. For example, they may not yet know the words 'half' and 'mayonnaise'. The whole idea is that they should be encouraged to guess the meaning on the basis of the clues in the pictures, their existing knowledge of the topic, or possibly the sound of the word.

Suggested procedures

- Hand out the picture sheets, keeping one for yourself.
- Give the children a couple of seconds to look at the pictures so that they know what is there.
- Hold your picture sheet so that it is facing them and ask them to look at you.
- Read out the first sentence and show that you are looking for the picture which matches:

TEACHER: You need a slice of ham, a roll, some lettuce, some butter and some mayonnaise. . . . Is it this picture? *(pointing to the wrong picture)* . . . or this one? *(pointing to another picture)* . . . or this one?

- When the children agree which picture it is, show them that you are going to write the letter alongside 1 . . . . . . on the sheet.

- Read out the next instruction, start searching for it as before, and let them tell you what number picture it is.
- Read out the third instruction, but this time make them decide for themselves which number picture you are talking about. They write down the number without telling you. (A quick glance at the papers of one or two children near you will tell you if they are getting the idea.)
- Carry on with the rest of the instructions, giving them time to find the right picture and write down the number each time.

Possible follow up	If the children can write, they might like to devise their own surprise sandwich. They can take the basic pattern of instructions from the board but choose their own ingredients. Let them use their imaginations, even if you would not like to eat the sandwiches they describe!
Other language you can practise with this activity	You can use this basic format of jumbled pictures for any sequence of sentences you like. For example, they could be simply a list of shops the children are asked to 'go to' and the things they are asked to buy:

Shopping list

1. First please go to the bakers . . .
2. . . . to buy some rolls.
3. Next, please go to the post office . . .
4. . . . to buy some stamps . . .
5. and post two letters to England.

etc.

Or the pictures could tell a story.

Activity **6** **Let's tell a story together**	You tell the story. They do the actions! It is an actively fun and simultaneously involving form of responding by doing.
Language focus in this example	The story actually practises prepositions but that is a very dull way to think of it!
Materials required	You can use any short story which has plenty of repetition and which contains plenty the children can mime. Here is one which all the children can mime at the same time, sitting in their seats. It is a version of a story called 'The Lion Hunt'. It is set out in two columns so you can see what prompts and actions might be useful.

Suggested procedures

First tell the story with pictures or symbols on the board.

TEACHER'S WORDS	SYMBOLS
We are going on a lion hunt.	
Off we go!	
First we walk along the path.	

Then we go over the bridge.

Next we go up the hill.

Then we run down the hill.

Next we walk across the swamp.

Now we walk through the long grass. . . .

. . . Wait a minute, whatever's this?
. . . It's got four legs. . . . It's got a
long tail. . . . It's got a big head. . . .
Help! It's the lion! Quick. . . !

(Now go back the way you came – but fast! Point to each drawing as you go.)

Through the long grass.
Across the swamp.
Up the hill. *(Remember you are going the other way!)*
Down the hill.
Over the bridge.
Along the path.
Home! Hooray!

Now sit down yourself and tell the story again, this time with the actions as follows. Get the children to copy the actions and do each one with you before you move on to the next stage.

TEACHER'S WORDS	TEACHER'S ACTIONS
We are going on a lion hunt.	
Off we go!	
First we walk along the path.	*Make walking noises on your knees with your hands, left, right, left, right.*

Then we go over the bridge.	*'Walk' on the desk to make the hollow sound of the bridge.*
Next we go up the hill.	*Slow down, it's a steep hill!*
Then we run down the hill.	*Speed up.*
Next we walk across the swamp.	*Make squelchy noises and lift your hands as if lifting them from something sticky.*
Now we walk through the long grass. . . .	*Part the long grass with your arms, making swishing noises.*
. . . Wait a minute, whatever's this? . . . It's got four legs. . . . It's got a long tail. . . . It's got a big head. . . . Help! It's the lion! Quick. . . !	*'Feel' each leg.* *Feel the tail.* *Feel the head.*

(Now go back the way you came – repeating the actions in reverse order – but fast!)

Through the long grass. Across the swamp. Up the hill. *(Remember you are going the other way!)* Down the hill. Over the bridge. Along the path. Home! Hooray!	*Slump in your chair and wave your hand in victory.*

Possible follow up The children could draw the story in their books using very simple symbols like those above. The drawings can then be used for later repeat tellings of the story as in the variations below. If the class can write, they could write the story out too to go with the pictures.

Variations
a) In this form, the story has been kept very simple so you may find one of the class would like to tell it instead of you. Leave the symbols on the board and practise them with the whole class first. Then choose a volunteer to come to the front and be the storyteller.
b) You can also turn this into pairwork with all the children taking turns to tell their partner the story while they both do the actions.
c) Best of all, get the children to make up their own simple story in pairs and teach it to the rest of the class.
You can make up your own story to practise almost any language you want.

Final comment This activity is very definitely a stirrer so think of something quiet to follow, like drawing the pictures as suggested above.

GROUP **2**

'Guess!'

The intention behind this group of activities is:

– to set up meaningful practice through real language use by providing the children with a good reason for going over and over the same items;
– to exploit the children's sense of fun and instinct to respond to a challenge;
– to stimulate the asking of questions.

Activity **1**
Guess what I've got on my promptcard **

In this activity the children cannot see the promptcard which has been chosen. They have to guess and work out by process of elimination. This is such a successful and easy activity to set up that it has already been mentioned several times in preceding chapters. Here it is in detail.

Language focus in this example

This time, the activity is being used to provide oral practice on the topic of the weather.

Materials required

– A set of drawings representing the phrases you want to practise. For example:

– Blutack or something similar which can be used to stick the cards temporarily to the board.

Preliminary work

This activity builds on oral work the children have already done but, even so, it is a good idea to 'warm them up' by some straightforward chorus and individual repetition of the phrases. This will also give you a chance to encourage the children to be accurate.

Suggested procedures

– Collect the promptcards into a pile and give the pile to one child who holds them so that the other children cannot see which card is on the top of the pile.
– Start the guessing yourself, so that you provide a model for the children to follow:

TEACHER: Is it raining?
CHILD WITH CARDS: No!
TEACHER: Is the sun shining?
CHILD WITH CARDS: No!
TEACHER (*to rest of class*): Guess!
ANOTHER CHILD: Is it snowing?

– When someone guesses correctly another child is allowed to choose a card and you start the process again.

Possible follow up/Variations

a) Simultaneous pairwork (oral)

The only slight disadvantage of the guessing activity as it is set out above is that the teacher usually enjoys it too and is tempted to remain the central figure instead of letting the children take over. So, once the routine and the materials are familiar, try to find ways of changing it to pairwork so that all the class are working at once.

Suggested procedures

Demonstrate what they have to do.

– Stick the promptcards on the board.
– Write a number alongside like this:

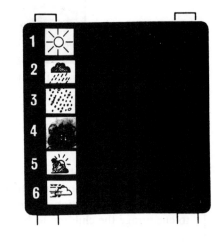

58

– Choose one of the promptcards and write its number somewhere on the board, concealing it so that the children cannot see what you have chosen.
– Get the children to guess which card you have chosen:

CHILD: Is it foggy?

TEACHER: No!

And so on until they guess correctly when you reveal the number you chose and wrote up.
– Set the children to work in pairs. Child A writes down the number of a card they have chosen.
– Child B starts to guess as before.

b) Simultaneous pairwork (written)

Another way to turn this activity into pairwork is to turn it into a written activity. We learn best when we use language to convey messages. Real written messages are quite hard to generate in the classroom so it is worth trying this.

The children work in pairs. Each child has a sheet of rough paper.

Suggested procedures

– Alongside each numbered picture on the board write the phrases they are learning.

– Each child decides on the word/phrase from the numbered selection on the board as in the previous activity.

- Both children in each pair write a question to find out what their partners have chosen.
- They exchange papers and underneath their partner's question they write their answer.

- They continue guessing in writing like this until one of them has successfully identified the other's choice. Most children like to keep a score of who gets the correct answer first each time.

Other language you can practise with this activity

In fact, this particular activity can be used to practise almost any piece of language because all you have to do is to think up the right question. For example, the children can guess by asking:

'Do you like?' + food
+ animals
+ school subjects
+ actions (e.g. swimming).

Or

'Have you got?' + personal possessions
+ brothers and sisters, etc.

Or

'Are you going to?'
'Have you?'
'Did you?'

The list is endless but it would help to look through the work you want to cover and to make your own list.

Final comment

One of the advantages of these guessing activities is that the children find their own level of language. This helps to build confidence. For example, it is possible for children to join in 'guess what I've got on my promptcard' when they only know one of the words. As the game progresses, they will hear the other phrases repeated and begin to learn them too.

The next example does not involve questions but is still based on guessing and on the same principles. It is something of a fraud, but maybe that is part of its appeal to the children. They certainly enjoy it!

Activity **2**
Telepathy

This activity is based on the idea of one child pretending to send a message to the others in the class by telepathy. The idea is to see how many people receive the message correctly!

This is another activity which is designed to make repetitive practice fun and a matter of real exchanges and interaction. It provides a reason for going over and over the same phrases. It can be done either as a totally oral exercise or it can make a very useful exercise for classes which are already writing.

Language focus in this example

As with all the best activities, it can be used to practise almost any phrase. In this example the topic is the days of the week.

Materials required

Some prompts for whatever you want to practise. In this example, they are letters written up on the board, but these prompts could also be pictures/symbols/words/sentences on the board.

Preliminary work

This activity builds on oral work the children have already done. Even so, as with most activities, it is a good idea to 'warm them up' with some quick chorus and individual accurate repetition before you start.

Suggested procedures

– Put the prompts on the board.

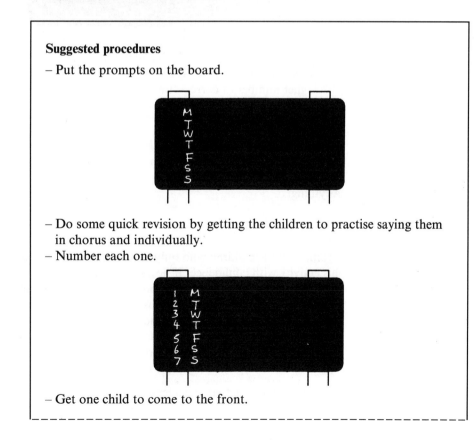

– Do some quick revision by getting the children to practise saying them in chorus and individually.
– Number each one.

– Get one child to come to the front.

– She whispers to you or writes down the number of the phrase she is going to 'transmit'.

– She is given a few seconds to transmit the message to the others by 'telepathy'.

– Each child in the class writes down the number of the phrase they have 'received'.

– Check *quickly* round the class, getting each child to say the phrase they 'received':

   FIRST CHILD (who wrote down 2): It's Tuesday.

   SECOND CHILD (who wrote down 4): It's Thursday.

   THIRD CHILD (who wrote down 2): It's Tuesday.

And so on.

– The child at the front can keep the score for each phrase alongside the prompts on the board:

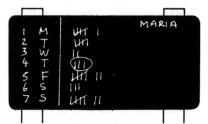

Maria chose to 'transmit' Thursday and scored 3.

– Repeat the whole process and let another child see if they can score a higher number of correct 'transmissions'.

Variation	You can use this to practise writing by getting the children to write the whole sentence down instead of just the number.
Other language you can practise with this activity	Anything!
Final comments	Again, even the children who only remember one phrase or word can join in this activity with confidence. If necessary, they can choose the same phrase each time. But they will hear the other phrases over and over again as the activity progresses, so they can soon start using those as well. What is more, the child who is 'transmitting' the message does not in fact have to say or write anything at all. Here is a chance for your least able pupils to take a central role! This is suggested here as a whole class activity but could equally, if not better, be done in groups once the children have the idea. The next guessing activity also lends itself well to pairwork.

Activity **3**

How many can you get right?

This activity is very like the 'guess what I've got on my promptcard' activity suggested at the beginning of this section. However, this time all the cards are laid out at the same time, face down, and the children have to see how many they can guess correctly out of the whole set.

The aim of this activity is again to provide repetitive but fun practice of whatever the class is learning at the moment. It is mentally engaging because it involves logical thinking as well as pure guesswork. It is also actually involving in the form suggested here because the whole class is working simultaneously in pairs.

Language focus in this example

This particular example is practising 'can' + verb.

Materials required

– Visual or written prompts.

– You will also need blutack or something similar if you are using visual promptcards.

Preliminary work

This activity would follow preliminary listening activities and repetition of the new phrases so that the class is already familiar with 'He can swim', 'He can ride a bike', etc.

Suggested procedures

– Stick or write your prompts on the board and number them.

- The class works in pairs.
- Child A writes down the numbers in any order he chooses and covers them so that B can't see.
- Child B guesses what the first number is by saying the phrase it represents:

  'She can swim.'
- Child A reveals the number and announces whether B was correct or not:

  'No, she can't./'Yes, she can.'
- Child B proceeds to see how many of the five he can get right.
- They keep a score then it is Child A's turn to guess and to see if he can improve on B's score.

Possible follow up   For classes that are already writing, you could move to a simple writing activity. Each child writes a list of numbers in any order they like and their partner writes out the sentences in that order. They then correct each other's list.

Other language you can practise with this activity   Anything you choose!

**Activity 4
Battleships**   This idea is based on a pencil and paper game called Battleships that children in England play in pairs. Perhaps you have your own version. In true 'Battleships', the two players each secretly mark on squared paper their fleet of ships. They then try to 'sink' their partner's ships by giving the coordinates for the squares where they think the ships may be. In this traditional form, the idea is rather limited as a language exercise, because all that the players say are the numbers and letters to give the coordinates. In the language learning version below, however, the coordinates are given by using phrases not numbers.

Again, the aim of this final guessing activity is to provide simultaneously involving, mentally engaging, repetitive real oral exchanges in a way which is also motivating and confidence boosting! It is the most complicated of the guessing activities suggested here and therefore is more suitable for the older primary children. However, it is enormously popular.

Language focus in this example   Food likes and dislikes.

Materials required   A small grid for each child in the class.

Alan	☺						
	☹						
Debbie	☺						
	☹						
Clare	☺						
	☹						
Hugh	☺						
	☹						

NOTE: If it makes life easier for you, there is no reason why the children should not draw their own grids, but it takes time so, if you are fortunate enough to have photocopying facilities, it is much simpler to draw the grids and duplicate them yourself. They do not have to be big. You can fit four onto a sheet of A4-sized paper.

Preliminary work

As this is a fairly complicated activity it is most suitable as a final practice activity, when the words or phrases are already very well established.

Suggested procedures

– Without letting their partners see, the children mark ten squares on the grid with a * in the top corner, like this:

Child A's grid:

Alan	☺						*
	☹	*	*				
Debbie	☺						*
	☹						
Clare	☺						*
	☹			*	*		
Hugh	☺					*	*
	☹				*		

Child B's grid:

		🥩	🐟	🥗	🍓	🍦	🍟
Alan	☺					✳	✳
	☹						
Debbie	☺						
	☹		✳		✳	✳	
Clare	☺		✳				✳
	☹			✳			
Hugh	☺						
	☹			✳			✳

– The children keep their grids hidden from their partners but try to find out what their partner has marked. So, for example, Child A 'fires' by asking the question:

'Does Alan like sweets?'

In this particular example a hit is scored.

– Child B answers:

'Yes, he does.'

and A marks it with a tick on her own card.

Child A's grid now
looks like this:

		🥩	🐟	🥗	🍓	🍦	🍟
Alan	☺					✔	✳
	☹	✳	✳				
Debbie	☺						✳
	☹						
Clare	☺						✳
	☹				✳	✳	
Hugh	☺					✳	✳
	☹					✳	

– It is now B's turn to 'fire' at one of A's choices:

'Does Clare like fruit?'

B marks the result on his card.

Child B's grid now
looks like this:

Alan	☺					*	*	
	☹							
Debbie	☺							
	☹		*		*	*		
Clare	☺		*					*
	☹			*	×			
Hugh	☺							
	☹			*				*

– The children continue with alternate questions until one child has found all the other's choices.

Variation	There is another form of this activity which ties in with maths work on intersecting sets. You will find it set out in detail in *Practical Activities 2* on page 154.
Other language you can practise with this activity	You can combine any two elements of information you like, for example: – Days of the week + hobbies to practise 'Do you swim on Mondays?' etc. – Furniture + rooms to practise 'There is a chair in the kitchen.' etc. (Notice that the children do not have to make questions. The activity can be done with statements.) Why not make your own list of the topics you most frequently need to practise and then see how many different combinations you can make out of them in this way?
Final comment	If the children in your class are not familiar with the game, it may take a little while for them to get used to it but once learnt, they will enjoy it.

GROUP **3**

'Get up and find out!'

The intention behind the activities in this group is to set up meaningful and real language interaction which involves movement round the room. Young children can become restless if they have to sit still for long periods. It is only fair to them and to us to provide them with the opportunity to move around. If we can do that, then they are more likely to be able and willing to sit still when we want them to! So, just as we wanted to exploit the desire to talk, we can also make good use of the desire to move.

Some of these activities involve more initial preparation than some of the others. However, they do repay the effort. For example, the materials made for the second and third activities in this group can be reused over several years.

Perhaps with some of these rather bigger activities it would be worthwhile sharing your resources with someone else. If there are other English teachers in your school, you could each produce a set of materials for one of these activities and then make them a common resource. You will, in any case, find that discussing these ideas with other teachers will stimulate other ideas and improvements of your own which are perhaps more suited to your circumstances.

The first activity, a class survey, is something you can easily set up on your own however.

Activity **1**
Interview grids ***

The idea of these interview grids is that all the children in the class conduct a class survey by interviewing each other. This kind of activity is very useful for encouraging real communication. Children can exchange real information about likes and dislikes, details of possessions, hobbies. If the question and answer work on these topics is only ever done by the teacher talking to the whole class at the same time, it is unsatisfactory in several ways. For a start, the activity tends to feel like a language learning routine rather than a real finding out and exchanging of information. Moreover, it has three particular drawbacks. The first is that only one child at a time is involved in answering. The second is that the children only produce the answers. They don't practise asking the questions. The third disadvantage is that each child is only likely to answer once at the most. Compare this with what happens in the activity below. By using a grid, you can turn the activity into simultaneous conversations which involve all the children in the class at the same time, and which require them both to ask the questions repeatedly and to give their answers repeatedly.

Language focus in this example

Conducting a class survey on likes/dislikes + animals.

Materials required   – For this activity, you need a grid for each child as in the example below, with several question prompts across the top (either written or drawn) and spaces at the side for the names of those interviewed.
                    – If you are going to demonstrate on the board what they should do, you will also need some blutack.

Preliminary work

Before the children are ready to do this exercise you will need to make sure of two things. Firstly, they need to have a reasonable chance of getting it right. So before you start this, you will want to provide some accurate practice of the words and phrases involved. (Remember that the children are going to be using the *questions*.) Secondly, the children must be clear as to how to do the exercise.

Suggested procedures

– Help the children to practise the answers by asking the questions yourself.
– Now practise the questions with them. You could just do some repetition work at this stage.
– Now begin to build up the grid on the board. As you and they are practising each item, stick or write it up in the position it will occupy in the grid.
– Draw the grid framework round the prompts.

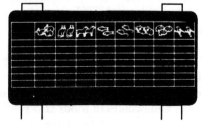

– Interview a child yourself, filling in the grid as you go.

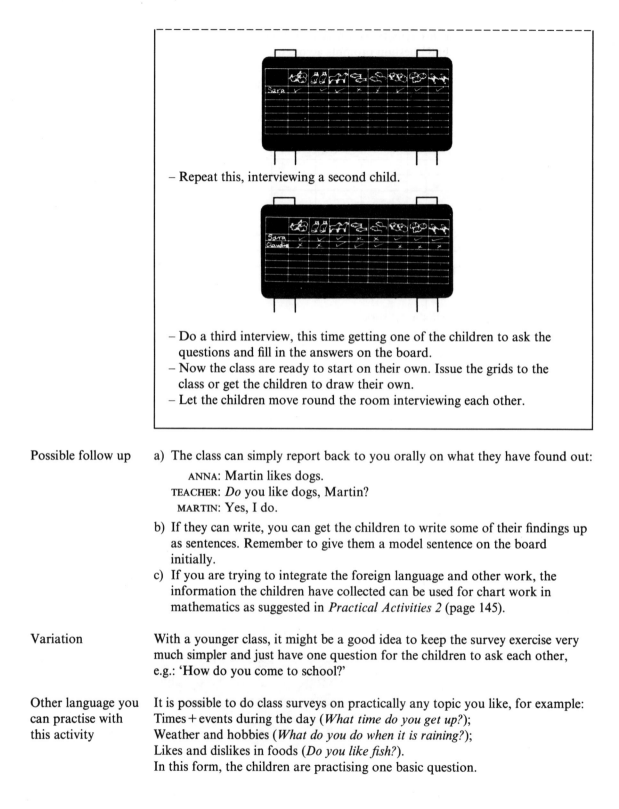

– Repeat this, interviewing a second child.

– Do a third interview, this time getting one of the children to ask the questions and fill in the answers on the board.
– Now the class are ready to start on their own. Issue the grids to the class or get the children to draw their own.
– Let the children move round the room interviewing each other.

Possible follow up	a) The class can simply report back to you orally on what they have found out: ANNA: Martin likes dogs. TEACHER: *Do* you like dogs, Martin? MARTIN: Yes, I do. b) If they can write, you can get the children to write some of their findings up as sentences. Remember to give them a model sentence on the board initially. c) If you are trying to integrate the foreign language and other work, the information the children have collected can be used for chart work in mathematics as suggested in *Practical Activities 2* (page 145).
Variation	With a younger class, it might be a good idea to keep the survey exercise very much simpler and just have one question for the children to ask each other, e.g.: 'How do you come to school?'
Other language you can practise with this activity	It is possible to do class surveys on practically any topic you like, for example: Times + events during the day (*What time do you get up?*); Weather and hobbies (*What do you do when it is raining?*); Likes and dislikes in foods (*Do you like fish?*). In this form, the children are practising one basic question.

It is also possible to practise clusters of questions which belong naturally together, such as personal details:

'Have you got a brother?'
'Have you got a sister?'
'How old are you?'
'Where do you live?'

NAME				

Final comments

i) If you have done this kind of 'get up and move around' work in languages before, you will know how effective it is. If it is a new technique for you, you may well be worried about how much English the children are actually talking. It is true that some children may be tempted to 'cheat' by using the mother tongue. In this respect, children are rather like water; they choose the easiest route. Our job is to make the route we hope they will follow easy enough to be worth trying. That is why practice beforehand is so important. It is also worth pointing out that even if they lapse occasionally into the mother tongue, ten minutes of simultaneous talk will have demanded more English from any single child than would occur in a similar teacher/child question and answer session with the whole class, however machine-gun-like its speed.

ii) This activity is perfectly feasible with a large class if there is room for them to move around. If your classroom is very cramped, you can limit the number of children on the move at any one time in the following way. Start with a smaller number of children on the move as interviewers. (I suggest ten but it depends on your classroom. In any case, you want as many children moving as is reasonable in your particular room.) Each of these children is allowed to interview three classmates and then has to sit down. Meanwhile, as soon as any child has been interviewed twice, they can get up and themselves become an interviewer. As soon as they have done their three interviews, they sit down again. This system also has the effect of making the children want to be interviewed so that they can get up and become one of those moving around.

iii) As regards accuracy, it is also true that not all the class will be getting the phrases exactly right. You may worry that you cannot get around and correct everyone. There are several things to say here. The first is that if you have practised the activity reasonably before you set the children to work independently, this is not likely to be much of a problem. Besides, you know your children. You know who to listen to first and whom you can leave to get on with the activity on their own. You can also offer the occasional correction as you go around if something is badly wrong or if the child looks as if they would be glad of help. But be careful not to break too heavy-handedly into what the children are doing. That is the second point. What matters in this kind of exercise is that the children concentrate on getting the message across.

Thirdly, you will also find that they correct each other. However, if you do find that the whole class is getting something disastrously wrong, then you can stop everyone, practise it briefly and then restart them.

(iv) You may also be concerned that the children's behaviour will deteriorate. You will discover that although the noise level must go up because they are all talking at once, they tend to get so involved in what they are doing that behaviour ceases to be a problem. In fact, this kind of activity is not just suitable for 'good' classes who behave well anyway, but is particularly appropriate for restless classes precisely because they will talk to each other whether we like it or not!

Activity **2**
Test your friends

This is another speaking activity which is based on the children's instinct and need to get up and move around. It gives them a good reason for doing so by building on their desire to talk to each other. It also provides a great deal of practice of a limited topic because each conversation they have is slightly different. In the process, it seems like fun rather than serious learning because it involves making and using something usually more associated with play than with school.

Making a 'fortune teller'

Language focus in this example

Numbers.

Materials required

A square of paper (21cm by 21cm is a convenient size) for each child and one for yourself (a bit bigger so they can see it clearly when you are demonstrating what to do).

Preliminary work

Listening and oral work on the numbers 1–10.

Suggested procedures

Stage 1: Making the 'fortune teller'

– Show the children what to do. They copy you at each stage. The English is very simple. It goes something like this.

TEACHER'S WORDS   TEACHER'S ACTIONS

Now, watch carefully.

First, fold your paper like this.
Press hard (with your thumb) like this.

TEACHER'S WORDS	TEACHER'S ACTIONS
Now, open it again.	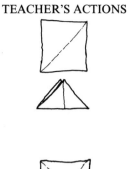
Next, turn it round. Now fold it like this.	
Open it. Now, watch!	
Fold it like this. Press hard with your thumb.	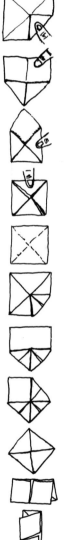
And like this . . . press hard.	
And like this . . . press hard.	
And like this . . . press hard.	
Now, watch carefully.	
Turn it over like this.	
Next, fold it like this . . . press hard.	
Now like this . . . press hard.	
Then like this . . . press hard.	
Then like this.	
Next, fold it like this. Yes! Press hard.	
Then like this.	

Now, watch . . .

(and you demonstrate how the fortune teller works).

Stage 2: Writing inside

– Each child chooses
  eight numbers and
  writes them on the
  flaps.

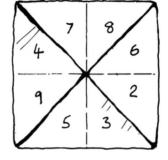

– The children then each make up eight sums with the numbers between
  1–10 and write those *under* the flaps.

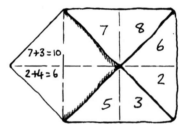

Stage 3: Testing their friends

– Show them first what to do by using a volunteer from the class.

TEACHER: Say a number.
  CHILD: Three.
TEACHER: *(makes 3 moves with the fortune teller, counting)* One, two,
    three.
TEACHER: Choose a number.
(The child chooses one of the numbers now revealed by the fortune teller.)
  CHILD: Five.
TEACHER: *(lifts the flap and reads out the sum)* What is five plus two?
  CHILD: Seven.
TEACHER: Yes.

When the children have got the idea, let them get up and test their
friends.

Variation	You can adapt this activity by altering the questions the children write under the flap.
Other language you can practise with this activity	You can make the questions general questions, such as: Where do you live? How old are you? Do you like . . .?
	Or, for a class that is learning to read and write English, the questions under the flap could test spellings on any topic you like, such as food, animals, parts of the body, colours. To make sure they start with the words spelt correctly on the fortune teller, the children can choose eight items from a list on the board. Getting them to practise spelling simple words to each other is, in fact, a good way to practise the alphabet in English.
Final comments	Notice that the demonstration of how to make the fortune teller is done in English. Simple demonstrations like this, which use limited language but a great deal of visual support, will help the children and you to get used to the process of doing things in English. Even a small task like this is a good example of real language use. Later in the book you will discover that apparently more complicated tasks in fact build on exactly the same techniques.

Activity **3** **Find someone who has the same card**	Like the previous activities, this is designed to provide simultaneous meaningful involvement.
	The idea is that the children have to find someone else in the room whose card of pictures or words is the same as the one they themselves have been given.
Language focus in this example	Pets: 'Do you like' + animals.
Materials required	Make a set of cards for the topic you are practising.

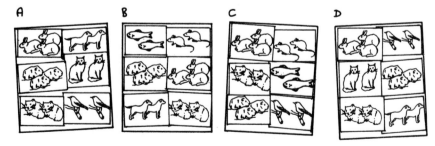

All the cards are based on the same group of items, but the exact selection on any one card only matches one other card in the set, i.e. in the above example, card A matches card D, although all four of the cards have several pictures in common. You need enough cards for all the class, so for a class of thirty children you will need fifteen pairs of cards.

Preliminary work

This activity will come towards the end of your work on any topic. For example, it would follow on well from the interview grid which has just been suggested. So, this example uses the same pictures as the interview grid in order to remind you that many of the activities in this chapter can be combined to create very full but varied and enjoyable practice of one set of phrases.

As with the interview grid, you need to practise the questions and answers carefully beforehand, so that you can let the children get on with it on their own once the activity starts. It can also help to have one or two key sentences on the board. You will find that the more able children will ignore them, the middle ability children will look occasionally for reassurance, and the least able will look every time.

Suggested procedures

You will need to demonstrate how to do the activity. As you can see in the suggested procedure below, the technique of demonstrating is basically the same as in the fortune teller example above or the paired reading example of how to teach in the target language on page 17.

– Take two pairs of cards from the pack.
– Keep one card yourself. Give the other three cards to three children, keeping a careful mental note of which child has the card that matches yours. (Finding the easiest route is also allowed for the teacher sometimes!)
– Make a statement about your card saying:

  'I like hamsters. Do you?'

– If the child you are addressing also has a hamster on their card, they will reply:

  'Yes, I do!'

– Carry on asking, until it is clear that your two cards do not match.
– Ask the next child. Leave the third child who *has* got your card till last, by which time the class will have got the idea that you are looking for the matching card.
– Take back all the cards, reshuffle the pack, issue one card to each child in the class, and tell them to 'find your partner'.

Possible follow up

As a final settling activity to calm the class down again after all the wandering around and talking to each other, the children could choose phrases from their cards and write them in their books.

Variation

There is no need for the prompt to be a picture card if the class can read. It could just be a list of words.

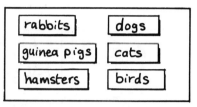

Other language you can practise with this activity

To make economical use of your preparation, one set of cards can be used to practise other different language exchanges on other occasions. For example, the cards above could also be used to practise 'I have got . . .' or 'I can see . . .'.

You can also produce a different set of cards to practise other language such as 'going to' + places:

'I am going to the cinema. Are you?'

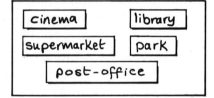

Or 'I like' + hobbies:

'I like swimming. Do you?'

Final comment

You can make these cards yourself or get the class to do them for you. First you need to work out the combinations of prompts for each pair of cards. Here is one way to do it.

To work out the card combinations:

– Choose which language items you want to practise. Each pair of cards will need at least five prompts. So work out your system along the following lines (worked out here for eight items to give five per card).
– Allocate each prompt a letter of the alphabet.

Prompts:

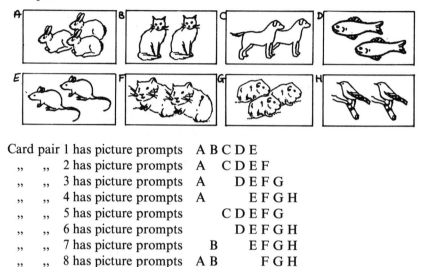

Card pair 1 has picture prompts   A B C D E
    ,,   ,,   2 has picture prompts   A   C D E F
    ,,   ,,   3 has picture prompts   A   D E F G
    ,,   ,,   4 has picture prompts   A   E F G H
    ,,   ,,   5 has picture prompts   C D E F G
    ,,   ,,   6 has picture prompts   D E F G H
    ,,   ,,   7 has picture prompts   B   E F G H
    ,,   ,,   8 has picture prompts   A B   F G H

and so on until you have enough card pairs for a class set.
– One sheet of A4 thin card will provide eight cards. You can cut up the prompts and stick them on the cards yourself. Alternatively, you could turn the preliminary work into a reading exercise, give the children the words to be written on the cards, and let them cut the pictures out and stick them on.

Activity **4**
Poster search

The basic idea behind poster searches is that children are given a set of questions to answer. The information they need to answer these questions has been put up on posters round the room. The children move around, searching for the answers.

This is another way of providing a valid reason and necessary opportunity for the children to get up and move around. It is also another activity which demands considerable preparation but, again, the materials required will last for several years. Again, it would be worth sharing the preparation and the end product with other teachers if you can.

Here are two examples which work in slightly different ways. The first is the easier version of the two, both for you to prepare and for the children to do. The list of things to find out is in English and the posters are simply pictures of people with speech bubbles containing drawings.

Language focus in this example

Weather.

78

Materials required — You need five or six largish backing sheets of plain paper (the reverse side of old wallpaper is one cheap possibility) to make a series of 'posters' relating to the topic you are practising. These examples were made by cutting pictures of people out of magazines. The 'speech' bubbles and names were first drawn on plain paper then cut out and stuck on to the posters:

— You also need a question sheet for each child. In this case, the questions are in the form of multiple choice because in this way they repeat the reading the child has to do.

```
                              Name........  Class.....
        What are they saying?
        Richard is saying: it's raining.        □
                            it's a nice day.     □
                            it's windy.          □
                            it's hot.            □

        Ian is saying:      it's cold.           □
                            it's a nice day.      □
                            the sun is shining.   □
                            it's raining.         □

        Janet is saying:    it's snowing.        □
                            it's raining.         □
                            it's foggy.           □
                            it's hot.             □

        Cathy is saying:    it's raining.        □
                            it's cold.            □
                            it's snowing.         □
                            it's windy.           □

        Malcolm is saying:  the sun is shining.  □
                            it's raining.         □
                            it's snowing.         □
                            it's foggy.           □
```

Preliminary work

As a reading activity, this will come towards the end of your work on the topic. It could follow preliminary reading work based on the idea of 'identify which one I'm saying'. For example:

– Draw (or stick) your visual prompts on the board.

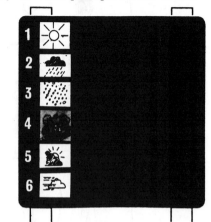

– Write the phrases up on the board alongside the visual prompts.
– Write a number alongside each one.

– Say one of the phrases and ask the children to write down its number.
– Do the same with the rest of the phrases. The children write down the numbers each time in the order you say them.
– Check quickly by giving them the numbers.
– Repeat the activity until they are all recognising the phrases confidently. At some stage, remove the visual clues so that the children are identifying the written words alone.

If they can do this, the children are ready to tackle the main activity.

> **Suggested procedures**
>
> – Pin or blutack up your poster sheets around the room. Space them out so that the children don't end up crowded together.
> – Issue the question sheet to each child.
> – Give the children time to read through the sheet so that they know what the questions are.
> – Read out one of the questions yourself. (Choose one from some way down the page so that the children can see that they do not have to start with question 1.)
> – 'Search' for the answer obviously, by going from poster to poster. When you have found it, let the children see you write down the answer so that they can see that this is what is expected of them.
> – Tell the class to get up and find out. (It is probably a good idea to start the children off at different points in the room so that they don't all cluster in one spot answering the first question.)

Possible follow up   If you like the class to write, the children can copy the correct answers into their books and draw a speech bubble clue alongside.

Variation   Instead of using speech bubbles, you could use pictures of objects. For example, here is a poster with six names in the middle and pictures of six objects around the outside. Each name is connected by a line to one of the objects. The children must find out who has which object.

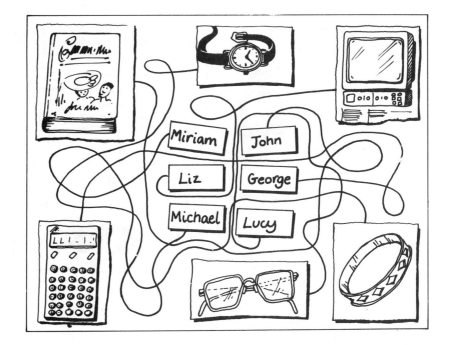

81

This poster could be one of a set about personal life. The other posters being about favourite foods:

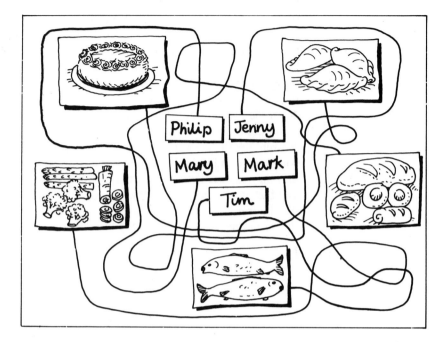

favourite colours, or animals:

and so on. The question sheet would be a multiple choice sheet like the one on the weather.

Other language you can practise with this activity

The only real limitations to the basic idea are your drawing skills or the pictures you can find to use. In theory, the activity can be used for any words or phrases you want to practise.

The second example of a poster search is probably suitable for older children only. Whereas the first example just involved looking for the *picture* to match the phrase written on the worksheet, this time the children are scanning the English on the posters for *information*. The activity in this form encourages intelligent guessing and confidence in partial understanding.

Language focus in this example

Shops and shopping.

Materials required

– For this particular topic, you can make your posters by drawing the basic outlines of shops in a street and then sticking up notices and advertisements on different coloured pieces of paper.

– You also need a question sheet for each child or pair of children. This time, the questions are single choice questions like:

'What do apples cost?'
'When does the cake shop close?'
'In how many shops can you buy bread?'
'Where are the cheapest lemons?'

(On other occasions, the questions can be in the mother tongue to enable more challenging things to search for. What matters is that the children scan the English 'text' on the posters.)

Preliminary work

As a reading activity, this will again come towards the end of the topic of shopping. Furthermore, as the activity is designed to practise scanning and you are not expecting the children to recognise or know every single word, this time you do not need to pre-check everything.

Suggested procedures

– As before, show the children what to do by reading out one of the questions and yourself walking round to find the answer. Show them how to write down the answer.
– Let the children get up and find the other answers.

Variations

These posters can also be on any topic you like. Here is a chance to introduce authentic materials. You could make some posters which use English advertisements. Or, if you visit England, you could take some photographs, for example of road signs, which would also make attractive and interesting posters.

    For once you would not have to worry that ordinary photographs which you yourself have taken are too small for the classroom. This time, the children are moving around and can get close up to them.

Final comments

i) As they are described here, the posters look complicated to make. Remember they can be reused on different occasions.

ii) The success of this activity shows in the fact that some teachers who have originally come across it as a language activity frequently adapt it for other subjects! So here is an example of a technique from language work which you can integrate into other areas of the curriculum. Even potentially boring facts can become quite interesting if they are written up on several sheets round the room and the children have to find the answers. There is one group of children who signalled their enjoyment of this activity by calling it a 'treasure hunt'!

GROUP **4**

'Can you remember?'

The activities in this group are intended to show that we can use memory to create real communication. In other words, the main concern is to increase mental engagement by giving the children a good reason to remember what they are saying, hearing, reading or writing.

Activity **1**
Disappearing prompts ****

In this activity, the children are initially shown a sequence of promptcards for which they say the appropriate phrases. The cards are then removed one by one until the children are saying the whole sequence from memory.

This is a simple activity which you can set up quickly. It gives the children a chance to recall the English directly. As well as providing a good reason for repetition, it appeals to the children's sense of fun and challenge. It is a good activity for the core repertoire.

Language focus in this example

'I am going' + the names of shops.

Materials required

– A set of prompts for the words or phrases you want the children to learn. In this case, they are just initial letters written on the board. Here, Bu = Butcher, PO = Post Office, N = Newsagent, S = Supermarket, F = Fish shop.
– On occasions when you use picture prompts, you will require blutack or something to stick them to the board.

Preliminary work

This kind of activity follows on well from some of the listening activities in Group 1 such as 'Write down the number' (page 41) or a 'Listen and arrange' activity (page 49).

Suggested procedures

– Write your prompts on the board. (Even if you are just writing them this time, it helps to draw a line underneath each one for reasons that will become clear.)

- Get the children to repeat them after you in sequence.
- Next the children practise saying the whole sequence while you just point. Keep them in sequence.
- When the children are familiar with the sequence, rub out a letter or prompt from the row.

- The children now say the sequence including the one that isn't there.
- Carry on removing items in stages until the children are saying the whole sequence entirely from memory. (It helps to touch the empty space on the board or the table as they try to remember. This is why it helps to draw a line under your prompt so that you and they can see where there is a space.)

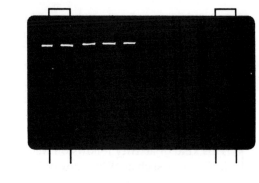

Possible follow up/Variations

Try to remove yourself from the centre of activity by inviting a child to the front to be teacher. You can also increase involvement by letting the children test each other in simultaneous pairs.

For a class that can read and write English, you can also turn this into a writing activity, in which case it could look something like this:

Suggested procedures

– Write up the phrases, but in a different sequence, on another part of the board and leave them there so that the children have a model in front of them.

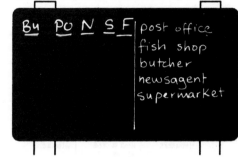

– Remove the prompts in the same way, one at a time, only this time the children have to *write* the sequence out from memory.

Other language you can practise with this activity

You can use this technique to practise any list of words, but it is even better if you can give the words a natural context such as 'I bought . . . .'.

In this way, you practise two things for the price of one while increasing the meaningfulness of the language being used. Other useful introductory phrases which you might also want to practise anyway are: 'I like . . . .', 'I don't often . . . .', 'I can . . . .', 'I have . . . .', 'I don't want to . . . .', 'I must . . . .', etc.

Final comment

As an oral activity, this provides plenty of actual and mental involvement although it is quite noisy. As a written activity, it is both settling and quiet.

Activity 2
Matching pairs **

For this activity the children work in pairs or small groups. They are given two sets of cards and have to find the matching pairs. In the form suggested here, the activity is designed to develop scanning skills in reading.

Language focus in this example

Describing what people are wearing: clothes and colours.

Materials required

For each pair or group of children you need an envelope containing a set of twelve picture cards and a set of matching statements. Below you can see an example of these before they were coloured and cut up into cards. You do not need to go to the expense of proper card. Cards made of ordinary paper seem to survive in the classroom.

She is wearing a green hat and a yellow dress.	She is wearing a yellow blouse and a red skirt.	He is wearing a green shirt and blue trousers.
He is wearing a blue shirt and yellow trousers	She is wearing a green hat, a blue blouse and a red skirt.	She is wearing a yellow skirt and a green blouse.
She is wearing a yellow blouse and red trousers.	She is wearing a blue hat and a red dress.	She is wearing a blue blouse and a green skirt.
He is wearing a blue hat, a red shirt and green trousers.	He is wearing a yellow shirt, blue trousers and a red hat.	She is wearing a yellow dress and a blue hat.

Preliminary work

This is a consolidation activity so, before the children start on an activity of this kind, you will want to have done plenty of listening, speaking and reading practice with them.

Suggested procedures

– First demonstrate how the activity works by playing a few turns with a child at the front.
– The children then work in simultaneous pairs or groups in the following way. They put the picture cards face down in a pile. The matching sentence cards are spread face down on the table.

- Child A takes the top picture card from the pile and turns over one of the sentence cards.
- Together the children scan the sentence card to see if it matches the picture.
- If the cards match, Child A keeps the pair. If the cards do not match, the picture card is returned to the bottom of the pile and the sentence card is turned back face down in its place.
- The next child has a turn.

The skill in the game lies in remembering where the various sentence cards were.

Possible follow up   When they have finished the game, the children can choose five matching pairs and write out the sentences. Later, they can draw the pictures to go with them.

Variation   One very effective variation is to combine *three* elements of information rather than just two (i.e. clothes and colours) as above. For example, you can have directions on one set of cards, the names of shops on another and a map with each set of cards, on which they have to follow the directions.

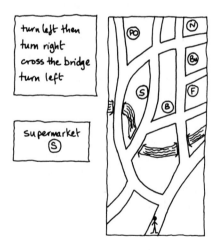

This time, the only way the children can tell if they have got a pair is to use the map to follow the directions on the first card they have picked up and see if they reach the shop on the second card.

| Other language you can practise with this activity | You can use this activity to practise a wide variety of language. It can be used just to practise vocabulary with a picture card and a word card. You could also use the activity for language associated with: |

Descriptions of people

Numbers

Weather

Actions

and so on.

| Final comments | i) You may still be uncertain about using the language you are teaching to show the children how to do the activity. You may be tempted just to tell them in their mother tongue. Remember, however, that they can understand better if they can *see* what to do. By talking to the children in simple English while they watch what you are doing, you are providing real language use and are building on and developing their confidence in working on partial linguistic information. If you would like some guidance on how to do this, you will find this particular demonstration written out in full on pages 17–18. |

ii) This is one of the activities that the children could help you to prepare. You can give them the word sheets and the picture sheets already drawn but not yet coloured in. They would have to read the word sheets and colour the pictures in correctly. This in itself is a very satisfying reading exercise, and all the more so because the children are preparing a game which they are then going to play. Alternatively, they could make their own game. Give them two blank sheets of paper. One for the pictures and one for the words. They can fill the sheets in themselves with the pictures and phrases of their choice. When they have finished, they can cut up the sheets and play matching pairs.

| Activity **3**
Silent dictation! | This activity comes at the transition between reading and writing. The children are briefly shown a phrase, word or sentence which they then have to write from memory. It is a very simple activity from the teacher's point of view, but demands a quite complex mental process from the children. It must be stressed that they are *not* remembering each part of each word. They are understanding the words and remembering *the message* which they then have to produce for themselves. |

Language focus in this example

Giving personal information.

As with all writing activities, it makes sense for the children to practise the kinds of things they will actually want or need to write and not just things they are more likely to want to say. So, in this example, they are using the kinds of statements they are likely to want to write in a letter to a penfriend.

Materials required

– You need some word cards (again paper will do) with phrases that you want to practise.

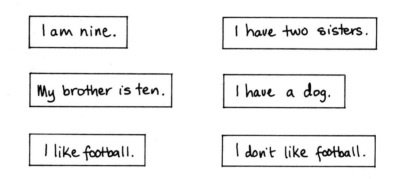

– Paper for the children to write on. Scrap paper will do.

Preliminary work

With all written work it is very important that the children have heard, said and seen the words many times before they come to write them. This activity comes late on in your work on a topic.

Suggested procedures

– The teacher holds up the word card or a sentence card without saying anything.
– After a *brief* pause, the teacher puts down the card and the children write down what was on it.
– It sometimes helps to give a second viewing but it is important to remember that they are *not* copying so don't show the phrase for too long.

Possible follow up

You could let the children copy into their books the list of words or phrases you write on the board. (This time you want them to copy so it is accurate!) They could then do silent dictation in pairs. It works like this:

– Child A is the pupil first and closes his book. He has a piece of scrap paper to write on.

– Child B opens her book, points to a word/phrase, counts to three under her breath and then closes the book.
– Child A has to write the selected word/phrase.
– After three turns, both children check how correctly A has written the words or phrases.
– They then change over and Child B becomes the pupil for the next three 'dictations'.

(It is suggested that they count to three or they will probably be tempted to show their friends the words for no more than a millisecond and you might have arguments on your hands!)

Variations

If you have a very able or slightly older class, you could do more complicated versions of this activity.

a) Single words into whole sentences.

e.g.: You hold up

footUp| *football* |

The children write **I like football**

b) Opposites

The teacher holds up a word card | *big* | in the same way as before but this time

the children write the opposite. **small**

Other language you can practise with this activity

This activity is suitable for learning to spell any words you want and is also useful for practising writing short phrases.

Final comment

This is one of those satisfying settler activities that calm a class down beautifully! It also makes a very good 'off the cuff' standby activity for those awkward five minutes you suddenly have left over at the end of a lesson. If you have no word cards prepared, you can write the words on the board and cover each one with a sheet of paper while the children are writing it.

Activity **4**
What did it say?

This activity has already been referred to several times because it follows on naturally from some of the previous activities. True/false statements or questions are used to test the children's memory of the information they have just had in front of them.

Language focus in this example

Possessions: 'have' + objects.

Materials required

A completed grid for each child. The example below is a grid which has already been used as a listening grid and filled in by the children in response to a series of statements from the teacher, e.g. 'Sheila has got a football and a television. She also has a cat. She hasn't got any brothers or sisters or a bicycle.'

	⚽	📺	🚲	🐱	👫
Sheila	✓	✓	✗	✓	✗
Adam	✓	✓	✗	✗	✗
Carole	✗	✓	✓	✓	✓
Alan	✓	✓	✓	✗	✓
Dorothy	✗	✓	✗	✓	✓

Preliminary work

Completion of the grid as a listening exercise as above.

Suggested procedures

– Let the class look at their grid for ten seconds to remember it.
– They turn the grid over and you make a statement like 'Sheila has a bike.'
– They have to tell you if it is true or false. They can do this in a variety of ways. For example, if they don't yet know the new phrases and you are still just using this as a listening activity, they can just say 'True' or 'False', or they can say 'Yes' or 'No' or, 'Yes, she has.'/'No, she hasn't.'
– If you want something a little more calming, they can write T or F on a piece of rough paper.
– Or if you want to wake the children up a bit, they can react physically with some agreed signal (left hand/right hand, or stand up/sit down).

Possible follow up

It is possible to move on from this to a written activity. The children stick their grids in their books. They then each write out ten sentences as a quiz and record the answers upside-down at the bottom of the page.

Variations

a) You can change it into pairwork.

– Child A acts as teacher, Child B as pupil.
– Child B turns over the grid so that it can't be seen.
– Child A makes a statement, e.g. 'Dorothy has got a bike', and Child B must indicate in some way as above whether that is true or false.
– The children take it in turn to make statements about the information, which their partner has to accept or deny without looking at the paper.

b) Alternatively, you can keep this as a whole class activity but change the roles round. *The class* can look at the information and offer statements. *You* are the one who has to remember whether the statements are true or false. On this occasion, they will probably want to keep a score of the number of times they catch you out!

Other language you can practise with this activity

Anything you like!

GROUP **5**

'Think for yourself!'

In languages, just as in other subjects, we need to leave the children as much mental space as we can to do their own generating and organising of ideas. This is the particular focus and intention of the activities in this section, and it ties in very closely with the need to engage the children mentally in a combination of language use and thinking. It is a vital part of the process of helping them to make the language their own, which is one of the priorities identified earlier.

Activity **1**
Listing ****

The children are being asked to group words according to categories.

The activity combines the mental engagement of thinking for yourself with actual occupation. It provides a good way of learning vocabulary and phrases in their written form, because it provides meaningful repetition and demands that the children handle the concepts, not just the words. It appeared earlier, in Chapter 3 (page 26), in the form of an activity for practising shops and shopping. Here it is again with a different topic.

Language focus in this example

Clothes and seasons.
This particular example asks the children to group various items of clothing under the time of year when they are likely to wear them.

Materials required

No special materials are required.

Preliminary work

This kind of writing activity follows on from plenty of practice in hearing, saying and reading the words.

Suggested procedures

– Ask the children to work in pairs to make a rough list of any words they know for clothes. Give them a couple of minutes to do this.
– On one side of the board collect together the words they have thought of. (This is your chance to spell their rough versions correctly. Simply write them correctly yourself, however peculiar their version has sounded and don't ask them to spell the words at this stage.)

    CHILD: Pulver.
    TEACHER: Good idea . . . pullover *(writes it up)*.

– When you have a reasonable list, read the words through quickly with the class so that they are reminded of the sounds before they write them. This will also give you a chance to check the meanings.
– Next, write the four seasons on the board as four headings:

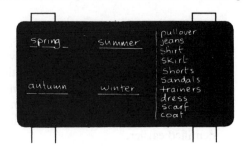

– Read one of the items of clothing from the list and ask the children when they wear it:

TEACHER: A pullover . . . . Do you usually wear a pullover in winter?
   CHILD: Yes. (*Teacher writes it on the board under the right heading.*)
TEACHER: (*Continues*) And do you wear a pullover in spring?

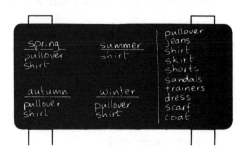

(Make it clear that things will come in more than one category.)
– Do a couple of examples like this and then set the children to write the column headings in their books and to copy the items into the column that *they* think is appropriate.

Possible follow up   The children could make their own little dictionaries in little booklets like those suggested at the end of this section on page 104. One column from the above exercise could become a page entry and the children could draw a little picture alongside some of the items.

Variations

The list does not have to be a dull, plain list of words. If you were practising rooms and furniture, the children could write their lists on a picture of a house:

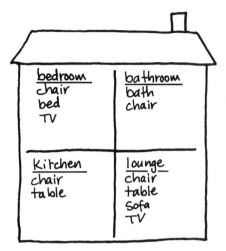

Or a list of sports could be written inside big weather symbols:

Or if they were making a list of what animals eat, they could write the words inside the animals:

Let the children use their imaginations. Remember, we want them to make the language event their own. For example, here is a house made like an advent calendar by an eight-year-old French girl. The lists of furniture are behind the doors and windows.

| Other language you can practise with this activity | It is quite fun working out combinations of categories and objects. Look through your textbook or syllabus to see what possibilities it offers, for example: |

Rooms and furniture   Weather and hobbies
Weather and seasons or months   Days of the week and school subjects
Sports and clothes   Colours and food, etc.

| Final comment | The children do not have to be able to write the words already to do this activity. In fact, it is intended to help them learn *how* to write them. So, when they make their rough lists, they can write the half-remembered words down as they like. This allows the children to take risks and draw on their partial knowledge in the way we are trying to encourage. They can, however, do it safely, because you are going to write the words correctly on the board a few minutes later. |

Activity **2**
Imagine

Instead of asking children to describe what you and they can both see, the idea of this activity is to stimulate them to find the words for what they imagine. We saw this on pages 7–8, where the children were given a picture of an animal's lair and asked to describe the monster they imagined lived down the hole.

Language focus in this example

In this present example, the children are going to make up a character and life for the child in the picture. In the process, they will practise the words and phrases they need to describe their own lives. This can be a purely oral activity or it can lead to imaginative written work.

Materials required

– You need one interesting, largish picture of a child for all the class to see.

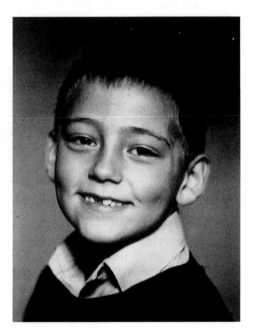

(The picture should be big enough for the children at the back of your classroom to see but they do not have to see all the detail because, remember, they are not going to describe the picture.)
– A collection of several small pictures of children. You can cut these from magazines and stick them on paper so that the edges don't get too worn and you can use them again.

Preliminary work

You will want this activity to be preceded by plenty of other work on describing families/hobbies/likes and dislikes, so it is a useful way of drawing together several topics.

Suggested procedures

Stage 1: It helps if you structure what the class are doing. You are going to leave the content and the end product to the children, but their imagination needs something to start it off. Total freedom is rather inhibiting! So . . .

– On the board write up question prompts for the kind of information the children are going to make up. For this example, they are going to think up a name for the child in the picture. They are going to imagine where he lives, who else there is in the family, what his hobbies are, and whether he has any pets. So the headings are: *Who? Where? Family? Hobbies? Pets?* (Once the children get the idea, they might like to suggest the topics themselves.)

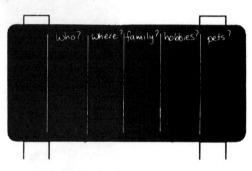

– Discuss the picture with the class, taking suggestions for the subject's name, where they live, etc. Take your time talking round the picture, reacting to and extending the children's suggestions if you can. The importance in the activity comes from exploring the possibilities:

TEACHER: What is his name? What shall we say? Nick? Brian?
(Suggests several to show there is no right answer.)
CHILD: Max.
TEACHER: Um . . . Max . . . that's a good name. OK. Has he only got one name? Perhaps he has two names . . . perhaps he has three names. Imagine . . .
ANOTHER CHILD: Stefan.
TEACHER: *(Writes up both names.)* OK. Max . . . Stefan.

Later:

TEACHER: Where does he live? . . . What shall we say?
CHILD: England.
(Teacher writes up 'England'.)
TEACHER: Is it a house or a flat? Imagine . . .
CHILD: House.
TEACHER: Oh, he lives in a house, not a flat, does he? Is it large or small? *(Writes up a child's suggestion.)* How many bedrooms has it got? Ten? That *is* big!

– As the children offer their ideas, write them on the board in note form so that the children can see what to do later when they are working on their own.

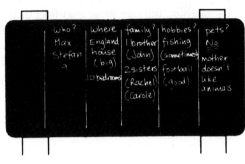

– In this way you build up a story on the board.
– When your notes are complete you can tell the story from them:

'This is Max Stefan. He is nine years old. He has one brother and two sisters. His brother is called John.' etc.

– Then get someone in the class to tell you the story too.

Stage 2: Having shown the children what to do, you now want them to work on their own in simultaneous pairs or small groups.

– In their books or preferably (because this is rough work) on scrap paper, the children draw the starter grid and copy in the headings.
– Give the small pictures out to the pairs.
– The children talk in pairs and agree on a story for their picture. You can go round and help them.
– When they have finished, choose one or two pairs to tell their story to the others in the class. You can make more of this by noting their versions on the chart on the board as they offer them.

Possible follow up/Variations

a) You can make more of the opportunities for oral work which this activity provides if you get the children to pass the pictures to another pair when they have finished their own story. In this way, each pair creates a life for more than one picture. If you do this, number the pictures for easy reference. The class can then compare ideas:

PAIR 1: This girl is called Anna.
PAIR 2: No, she isn't. She is called Jane.
        etc.

b) You can extend the activity in another way by getting the pairs to write up their story. They could write it in their exercise books or they could turn it into a little story book as the next activity suggests.

c) Another variation would be to get the children to imagine a conversation. You could find a picture of two people talking. For example, you might find something fun like these drawings of two imaginary beings. The children invent a conversation, perhaps on the topic you are practising at the moment. You can make this a regular feature of classwork by using it as a way to round off a topic or unit in a textbook if you are using one. If you have a classroom of your own with wall space where you can put up the children's work, this could make an interesting display.

Other language you can practise with this activity

This kind of activity lends itself to descriptions (as the monster in its hole, pages 7–8) and personal details (as in the example above). You can also use it to encourage the children to tell a story about an imaginary day excursion. For example, start with a picture of a place like the seaside or a big town, perhaps on a travel poster. Or, if you cannot find a big poster, you could give each pair of children a postcard or photo.

The prompt questions on the grid could then be:

When?	Day, month, time.
Who?	Remember that this is an exercise in imagination. There does not have to be anyone in the actual picture. The children can write themselves into the story if they want to.
Why?	A reason for going, e.g.: 'It is my birthday.'
What is going to happen?	'I am going to swim.'

Final comments

i) By asking the children to make up their own story instead of just getting them to describe what they can already see, you are creating real language use, which is one of our priorities.

ii) Do not worry if they use a mixture of foreign language and mother tongue in the notes and discussion. This doesn't matter. They are only preliminary rough notes to act as a prompt for oral feedback which will be in English.

iii) If you have some children in your class who are not very confident or able, *you* can tell the story in English from their rough notes, so that they feel they have played a full part in the lesson.

Activity **3**
Writing booklets

The idea of this activity is to get the children to make their own little booklets for their class.

Language focus in this example

Describing their home town or village.

Materials required

You can make each booklet out of two sheets of A4 paper. Fold the sheets into four, staple them down one of the long folded edges, and cut them to provide a quick, attractively-sized, sixteen-page booklet. You could, of course, get the children to make them for you at some point in a handicraft lesson. This is all part of making sure that language work is not isolated from the children's other work. The first time you do this activity with them, it may help to have a finished model to show what they are going to do.

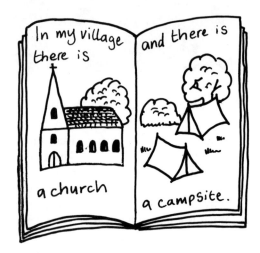

Preliminary work

This activity would come at the end of a topic when the class has already had plenty of practice on the topic.

Suggested procedures

– When the children are thoroughly familiar with the phrases in spoken and written form, write the key phrase on the board. In the example illustrated above the key phrase would be:

'In my village there is . . .'

– On *rough* paper, they make their lists of twelve things they will include in their booklets. Choosing twelve leaves enough room in the booklet for the much decorated title page and a 'hard words' list at the end.
– You could help them by discussing as a class what they might like to include and writing it up on the board for reference.

– When they have made their choice of items, the children have their spelling checked by you.
– They copy up the checked sentences into their booklets.
– They can then do the illustrations. (If you let them start with the illustrations, some of them will never reach the writing!)

Possible follow up

When completed, these booklets can be hung on the wall or put in a class library box to provide material for early finishers or quieter moments.

Variations

a) The children could make little workbooks to practise a particular structure, e.g. 'How many . . .?' or 'Do you like . . .?' They write the answers at the back of the book.

b) The children could also write up a small story based on a picture as in the previous activity.

Other language you can practise with this activity

You can use this activity to practise writing the kinds of personal things the children might want to write to a future penfriend, e.g. 'Me', 'My house', 'My family'. (Some children might like to use photographs instead of drawings to illustrate them.)

Final comment

You may prefer some classes to do the neat version of their writing on bits of paper which they then stick onto the pages of the booklet they have made. The advantage of this is that it allows for things going wrong without spoiling the whole booklet. The disadvantage is that it means you have to deal with the glue!

Activity 4
Design your own sticker

Most children seem to love badges and stickers. Why not get them to design their own? In doing this, they are expressing a genuine personal opinion or enthusiasm and in the process they are producing their own individual phrase in the foreign language. What they write is theirs. It is not an answer to a teacher's question. It is not an exercise where everyone in the class is trying to produce the right answer. The children can make up something that no one else in the class has thought of.

Language focus in this example

The example below is intended to encourage the children to use colours and to combine them with any other words which they choose.

Materials required

– Circles of plain paper. (You can get the children to make these if you like.)
– Coloured pens or pencils.

Preliminary work

This would make a good final activity in a sequence on colours.

Suggested procedures

– Tell the children what they are going to do. (If you have a sticker to show them it will help.)
– Draw a big circle on the board so you can design a sticker as an example.

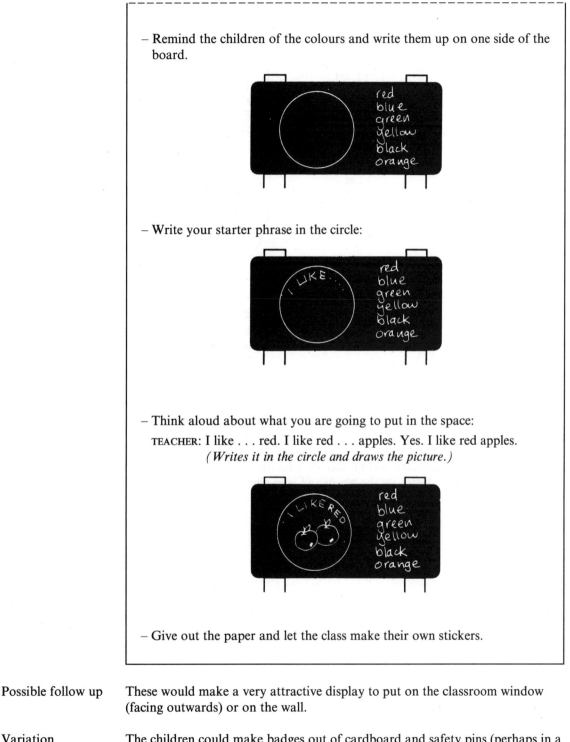

– Remind the children of the colours and write them up on one side of the board.

– Write your starter phrase in the circle:

– Think aloud about what you are going to put in the space:

TEACHER: I like . . . red. I like red . . . apples. Yes. I like red apples.
(Writes it in the circle and draws the picture.)

– Give out the paper and let the class make their own stickers.

Possible follow up These would make a very attractive display to put on the classroom window (facing outwards) or on the wall.

Variation The children could make badges out of cardboard and safety pins (perhaps in a handicraft lesson) and stick small circles of paper onto them to make personal badges.

Other language you can practise with this activity

Any short phrase which the children can combine with other language of their choice:

'I like' + sport
+ pop stars
+ food
+ animals

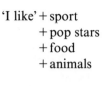

Or: 'I am' + adjective
+ age

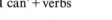

Or: 'I can' + verbs

Final comment

The children may ask for words they don't yet know or perhaps words you don't know. It doesn't matter. In fact, it can provide a useful introduction to dictionaries and their peculiarities. Any new words which come up can be written on the board and later shared with the whole class.

Activity **5**
Logical puzzles

The last example in this section is the most difficult and is really only suitable for the top of the primary range. In this activity, the children have to solve a logical problem. To do this they have to do more than just understand the words. They have to work out the implications of what they read.

Language focus in this example

Shops and shopping.

Materials required   A problem sheet for each pair of children.

Derek, Ann, Rob and Richard all go into a big shop. They each go to a different floor of the shop. One buys some sweets, one buys some pencils, one buys a book and one buys a tee shirt. Can you work out: What does Derek buy? Where does he buy it? What does Ann buy? Where does she buy it? What does Richard buy? Where does he buy it? What does Rob buy? Where does he buy it?

We know some things already.

1. Derek goes to the first floor.
2. You can buy pencils on the fourth floor.
3. Rob goes to the second floor.
4. Ann buys a tee shirt.
5. Derek does not buy sweets.

Use the grid to help you find your answers.

floor	who?	what?
1		
2		
3		
4		

Suggested procedures

– Give out the problem sheets and let the children try to read them for themselves first.
– Quickly draw the grid on the board.
– Read the text to them slowly.
– Enter the first piece of information (Derek goes to the first floor) on the grid on the board so that the children can see what they have to do.

floor	who?	what?
1	D	
2		
3		
4		

– Let the children work it out in pairs.

109

Other language you can practise with this activity

You can combine any three elements of information you choose and make a different puzzle for another occasion. You can reuse exactly the same format if you like. In the following example, the activity has been changed to practise people and possessions. (The names have been kept the same so that you can see how the formula has simply been transferred.)

The animals have escaped!

Here are four children called Derek, Ann, Rob and Richard. They live in these four houses. They each have a pet. One has a dog. One has a rabbit. One has a white mouse. One has a cat. The animals have got out. Can you work out: Whose cat is it? Which house does it come from? Whose dog is it? Which house does it come from? Whose rabbit is it? Which house does it come from? Whose white mouse is it? Which house does it come from?

We know some things already.

1. Derek lives at No. 1.
2. The rabbit comes from No. 4.
3. Rob lives at No. 2.
4. Ann has a cat.
5. Derek does not have a dog.

Final comment

Not everyone finds this kind of logical puzzle easy. That is why this variation uses exactly the same format as the original activity! If you need to use a different pattern, you can find puzzles like this in children's puzzle books. You will also find other ideas in them which you can adapt to the language classroom.

> This first selection of practical activities has shown how we can give our priorities real form in the materials we choose and the kinds of learning experiences they offer. However, in order to be effective, any activity needs to be set within a coherent overall framework. The second half of the book looks at the kinds of decisions and choices teachers have to make when creating a language programme or when implementing a programme they have been given.

PART II

Programmes and patterns of work

Introduction

Some teachers are required to work very closely to a given syllabus. Some more or less have to create their own programmes within rough guidelines. Others have to create the whole programme for themselves. Whatever our circumstances, that is to say, however much external guidance or control there is of what we teach, we always have to make choices at some level about what happens in the classroom. Having identified our priorities and their practical implications in Part I, we are now in a better position to make consistent and effective choices rather than haphazard decisions.

The priorities and realities discussed in Part I will help teachers to decide if, why, and how to adapt their programme or coursebook, if they have one, to suit particular classes. They will also underpin any decisions we make about creating our own schemes of work. Finally, they imply the steps we can take to integrate language work and other work in the curriculum. These concerns provide the topics for the three chapters in this second part of the book. This section, like the first, ends with detailed practical suggestions for classroom activities.

4 Working with a coursebook.
5 Working without a coursebook.
6 Integrating language work and other subjects.

Practical Activities 2.

4

Working with a coursebook

This chapter looks at three aspects of working with a class coursebook:

- choosing a book;
- supplementing the book if necessary;
- planning your progress through the book.

There are two common but extreme attitudes to coursebooks. The first is that it is wrong to deviate to any appreciable extent from what you have been given. The second is that it is wrong not to! Not only are both of these views unhelpful, they have also missed the point. The question is not 'Is it a good idea or a bad idea to use a coursebook extensively?' The important questions are 'What does the coursebook do well?' and 'What does the teacher do better?' When we have answered these questions we can each decide to what extent using a coursebook will suit our particular circumstances, what kind of coursebook will be appropriate for us and our classes, and how best to use it.

4.1
What a coursebook does well and what a teacher can often do better

The coursebook helps the teacher by providing:

- a clearly thought out programme which is appropriately sequenced and structured to include progressive revision;
- a wider range of material than an individual teacher may be able to collect;
- security;
- economy of preparation time;
- a source of practical teaching ideas;
- work that the learners can do on their own so that the teacher does not have to be centre stage all the time;
- a basis for homework if that is required;
- a basis for discussion and comparison with other teachers.

The coursebook helps the learners by providing a teacher who is more secure because of all the above. It also offers the learners:

– a sense of purpose, progression and progress;
– a sense of security;
– scope for independent and autonomous learning;
– a reference for checking and revising.

Together these make quite an impressive list of advantages. No doubt you could add others. However, there are several things that the teacher can often do better than a book, which are vital to successful language teaching and which tie in very closely with the priorities identified in Chapter 2. For example, the teacher is usually much better than the coursebook at:

– providing the spoken word in spoken exchanges;
– adjusting work in response to the reactions of the children;
– using communication other than words and pictures to back up language elements;
– setting up learning activities which encourage learners to talk and profit from interaction.

We need to keep these points in mind when choosing a coursebook.

4.2 Choosing a coursebook

Choosing a book for whole class use is always something of a leap in the dark. It may well be that you will not have a really good picture of its suitability until you have been working through it for some time. However, identifying the potential strengths of coursebooks generally, as above, can give us a starting point for looking at the strengths or weaknesses of any specific book. On this basis, we can make ourselves a list of questions about a book we are considering. If you set the questions out as a chart which you complete by blocking in a score from 1–5 (1 is poor, 5 is very good) you can get a clearer picture of the potential of any book. By dealing with several books in this way, you then have a comparative basis for making a decision.

What does this book offer?

FROM THE POINT OF VIEW OF THE TEACHER	1	2	3	4	5
A Do the book's priorities match with your priorities? e.g: If you take learning through communicating as your priority, does the book aim to set up genuine interaction? Real language use?				/////	
B Does the book seem to do what it claims to do? e.g: If it claims to set up real language use, does it provide pairwork which really involves communication and not just learnt dialogues?					/////
C Is it clear how to use the book?				/////	

	1	2	3	4	5	
D Is the book clearly structured and sequenced?				▨		
E Does it provide integrated revision of key items?					▨	
F Are there additional materials provided which you personally can't otherwise obtain? e.g: Authentic materials? Native speaker tapes?	▨					
G Does it offer lots of practical ideas?		▨				
H Does the book develop a balance of the language skills of listening, speaking, reading, writing which suits your needs?				▨		
I Does it provide plenty of varied practice of any one set of language items?			▨			
J Does it help you to set tests if they are required by your school?	▨					
K Does it manage to avoid sexual, racial and cultural stereotypes?	▨					
FROM THE POINT OF VIEW OF THE CHILDREN:						
L Does the book look interesting and fun?			▨			
M Can the children easily see what they have to do?				▨		
N Does the book provide much for them to do independently?		▨				
O Does it give them activities and tasks which are interesting and worthwhile in themselves and which are not just language exercises?				▨		
P Does it provide plenty for those children who cannot yet read and write with confidence?			▨			
OTHER QUESTIONS OF YOUR OWN:						
Does it						
Does it						
Does it						

The point about making and blocking in a chart like this is that it allows us to see where the strengths and weaknesses of any one coursebook lie far more clearly than we can do by just answering the questions in our heads. We can then match the results on our chart up to our individual circumstances and needs. In the above case, for example, the book is clearly strong in a majority of key areas. The weakness in question F might not matter very much if you and your learners have good contact with native speakers and culture through other channels such as tourism, television and pop culture. Similarly, the setting of tests (question J) may not be relevant in your particular case. On the other hand, if you did choose this particular coursebook, you would now be aware that you would have to counter the stereotyping it presents (question K). In any case, you would want to apply this system to more than one book before you finally decided on a coursebook.

Clearly, when it comes to working out the significance of results shown in the chart, you will need to ask yourself some questions both about yourself and the learners you will be working with. For example:

– *Are you working within a system which requires you to cover certain topics?* If so, the first and most obvious concern is to look at the coverage of these provided by the book. The next question then follows.
– *Are you sufficiently confident about your own use of the language to be able to provide any missing elements?* If so, the question of coverage is less significant.
– *Do you have lots of teaching ideas yourself or will you rely on the coursebook for ideas?* If you are going to be relying on the coursebook, then a poor score in question G is significant no matter how attractive the book is in other ways. Some books provide excellent basic material but leave you to sort out how to teach it. If you are not getting help from elsewhere, such a book may not suit you.
– *Does your school expect you to provide homework?* If so, you might want to make sure the book has things in it which you could use for this purpose and preferably has suggestions to make about what the homework should be.
– *Do your children have to buy their own books?* If so, price becomes a major consideration and would be one of the questions you would add to the chart.
– *How much time have you got for preparation of supplementary materials?* Good language teaching will often demand some extra preparation by the teacher, but there is no point in committing yourself to more than you *know* is realistic. If you have very little time to spare, you will give priority to a book which already provides plenty of practice of each topic.
– *Are you yourself confident with the grammar but not the sound of the language?* If that is the case, you may want to give priority to a coursebook which is accompanied by cassettes.
– *Are the children well intentioned but very slow?* In that case, again, you will be looking particularly for something that provides varied practice of the same things.
– *Are you going to use the book with one of the more difficult classes you have encountered?* Your priorities here would probably be attractively presented materials and ones which were simple and clear. Already restless children do not wait long to be persuaded that the work is worthwhile, and if they cannot immediately get into an activity, they are more likely to become silly.

– *Are there many children in the class who are weak at reading and writing?* If so, you must consider choosing a book which does not rely too heavily on words or on your explanations of them to show what is to be done. The answer to question P becomes particularly significant however much the book appeals to you in other ways.

If you ask yourself these kinds of questions and complete a chart like the one above, you are unlikely to make a bad choice of coursebook. However, it would be even better if you could discuss the matter with another teacher or a group of teachers. First you should agree on the questions for your chart. Then, ideally, each of you would fill in the chart independently for two or three books agreed on in advance. After that, you could discuss points where your judgements are the same or differ. You could follow this by discussing which elements you consider essential and which of them you are willing to compensate for. Finally, you could exchange ideas on how to compensate for the books' shortcomings. Even if there is only one book easily available, or if you have had the choice made for you, it is worth filling in a chart because it can give you a clear overview of the book you will be using and the demands it is going to make on you.

However, even if we have been fortunate enough to be able to choose our own books, most of us find ourselves at some stage working with a coursebook which is not totally suitable. This is particularly true when it comes to setting up real language use. As we have seen, this is something the teacher can usually do better than the book. Coursebook writers have a real problem here. The printed page is a very difficult medium for setting up genuine interactive work. The majority of books in schools still have not found a way round the problem. The teacher, on the other hand, is in a position to set up real communication much more easily than the average coursebook can. The book can provide the material but it is usually the teacher who can best organise the events which turn that material into a real language exchange.

4.3
Increasing the real interaction and communication offered by a coursebook

Here are two brief examples to show why it may be a good idea to adapt some coursebooks slightly and to remind you of how it can be done fairly simply by using activities like those in the preceding section.

Coursebooks often use a series of pictures like this to introduce the new words or phrases they are practising.

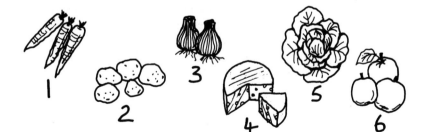

On the page, the exercise then often looks something like this:

Exercise A

Make up questions for each picture.
e.g. *Do you like carrots?*

The children go through the exercises making up a question for each picture in turn. (So far so good.) The problems, though, are firstly that the children only say each question once. Secondly, the element of true interaction is slight. Most importantly of all, the language is just a response to the pictures, it is not part of a genuine act of communication. However, it is possible for the teacher to use the same exercise from the book but to give it a little communicative 'twist'. If you have just read *Practical Activities 1*, you will know that it would be easy to use these same pictures to practise question formation as real language use by turning the exercise into one of the 'guess' activities. For example:

Guess which picture I'm thinking of

– Get a child to choose a picture without telling you or the class which it is. They can write down the number.
– Start guessing to show the class what to do.

    TEACHER: Do you like onions?
      CHILD: No, I don't.
    TEACHER: Do you like cheese?
      CHILD: No, I don't.

– Now get the class to help by asking their own questions. When they have guessed what the first child has chosen, let someone else choose a picture. After a while, this adapts very easily to pairwork with the children taking it in turns to guess what the other child has chosen.

You will be surprised how long the children will happily go on doing this. Compare it with the exercise provided by the coursebook where, once done, any repetition becomes empty and boring.

Although the exercise in its altered form sets up a genuine act of communication between the children, it is still an exercise not a genuine exchange of information.

Your book probably sets up pairwork. For example:

Exercise B

Work with a partner. Find out what they like.
e.g. *Do you like carrots?*
      Yes, I do./No, I don't.

This is better because each child is genuinely finding something out about a friend, but the activity is still rather limited in its impact if you stay tied to the book, because again the exchange, if it is to remain genuine, can only be done once. However, it does not take much to turn this exercise into a class survey of the kind set out in the previous section (see page 68 for details), where the children get up, move around and interview each other. In this form, they practise both the questions and the answers over and over again and are still genuinely finding out something about their classmates.

You will find that most of the activities suggested in the previous section are designed to be based on or grow out of coursebook work in this way. However, you may well be fortunate in your coursebook and may, in fact, not need to alter or add very much. Indeed, unless you are working from a book which is overwhelmingly unsuitable, it is probably a good idea first time through to use a book very much as the author suggests. After all, a great deal of thought has gone into the writing of it. By doing what the author suggests, you can also discover what the book really does or does not do.

However, whether you do adapt the book or just basically teach it 'straight', you will in any case have to work out how to pace your progress through it.

4.4
Pacing your progress through the book

Some coursebooks will tell you roughly how fast to move through them, i.e. how many lessons they expect you to spend on a unit with the mythical average class. Often, however, you will have to make your own decisions. Some teachers like to play it by ear and to see how the learners get on. They tend not to move on until the children have fully mastered a section or they move on quickly because the children seem bored. This is an attractive idea because it appears to have the merit that it puts the child's needs first. In fact, you could just as well be creating difficulties for the children. If they have to continue their programme with someone else next year, particularly if this involves transfer to secondary school, it will not help them (or your successor) if you have either done lots of topics sketchily, because the children quickly got bored, or so methodically and exhaustively that you have not completed the course.

It is probably a good idea to work out the overall distribution of the work for the year, much as you probably have to for your other work schemes. Working out a schedule like this is not a matter of being too teacher centred or rigid. You are not saying that you will stop unit 6 on December 6th whatever has happened. You may decide that the children need longer. The point is that if you do decide to take longer than originally anticipated, you now know that you will have to look for another perhaps easier area which you will be able to do more quickly than anticipated. Similarly, if you find that you are covering ground very much faster than you expected, you can ask yourself whether you are giving the children enough opportunity to *use* the language as opposed to just 'covering' it. If the answer is still 'yes', then you have a chance to do something independently of the coursebook. You could, for example, explore the possibilities of integrating language work and other subjects along the lines suggested in Chapter 6. In this way, a rough schedule prevents us from getting into difficulties without noticing it, and helps us to take advantage of opportunities that arise. Contrary to the view you will sometimes hear expressed, predicting your timing is a sign of effective flexibility not rigidity.

You can do the initial time allocation as follows.

– Check first how long the book suggests you take over each unit. It may talk in terms of weeks or lessons, but either way it will give you some idea of what kinds of adjustments you are going to have to make for your circumstances.
– Divide the book into the number of school terms you have. You can perhaps allocate slightly more time to units at the beginning and the end of the book on the grounds that you and the class will need to get warmed up and that you will also need time for revision. (Don't forget, too, those elements of the school year which temporarily but effectively suspend serious study, e.g. religious festivals, school events, exams, special summer activities.)

The rough allocation over a three-term year for a book of twenty units could look something like this:

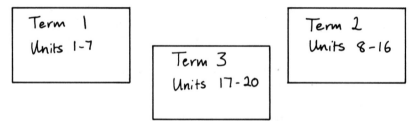

– Next do the same rough allocation for each half of the term. The outline scheme now looks like this:

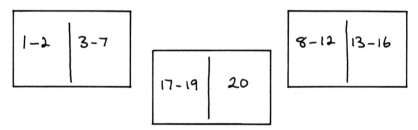

By now, it will be fairly clear that if you are to finish the book efficiently, you will have to do approximately x units in y weeks.

The consequences are clear. If you have little time each week for language work then you will have to put some of your preparation time and energy into identifying the essential items within the book and working out how to concentrate on those. If, on the other hand, you have plenty of time, your ingenuity will have to be directed towards working out how to provide plenty of additional and varied practice of the same topic. If the amount of time you take rests with you, you have a different set of decisions to make. Chapter 5 on working out your own programme discusses these.

> This chapter has looked at ways of shaping a coherent and effective programme around a coursebook. The need for coherence and structure becomes even more critical if you have to create the whole programme by yourself. Working without a coursebook is the focus of the next chapter.

5

Working without a coursebook

Many primary language teachers will have to work out their own programme in one way or another. Some teachers may have one coursebook as a resource book for themselves but none for their class. Others may have been given a syllabus in the form of a list of topics to work on in any way they choose. Some of you may have to work the whole programme out from nothing. This chapter offers one way of constructing your own work programme. It is suitable not just for teachers in schools, but also for those who are working independently. It would also be useful for those who are working with children under eight years old, for whom a formal syllabus is only rarely provided.

It is, in fact, surprisingly daunting to have the freedom to do what you like! However, the task is not as difficult as it may look. You will need to sort out three main things:

– How to give the programme a unifying thread and identifiable purpose.
– What topics to include and what to include under any particular topic.
– How frequent and how long language lessons should be if it is left to you.

We will look at each of these in turn.

5.1 Finding a unifying thread and purpose

Both teachers and learners need a programme which clearly has purpose and coherence. Learners need it because we all learn better if we can see what it is we are trying to do. This is for two main reasons. As learners:

– we need to know where to direct our energies;
– we need to have a mental framework into which we can fit new knowledge and understanding.

Teachers need a clear and coherent programme because:

– they too need to know where to direct their energies;
– it provides a central path through the otherwise limitless complexities of a language.

So the first task is to find a starting point and a unifying scheme. Luckily, in the language classroom, there is a very obvious and excellent starting point to hand; the children themselves. Taking the children as the starting point can both give our programme coherence and, at the same time, can help us in the second of our tasks, namely, sorting out what to include in that programme. Here is one way to approach the problem.

**5.2
Deciding what to include**

Stage 1: What aspects of life does a child really talk/think/read/write about?

Here are some suggestions. You will have others. Notice that these are not exactly topics. They are areas of interest, concern and experience.

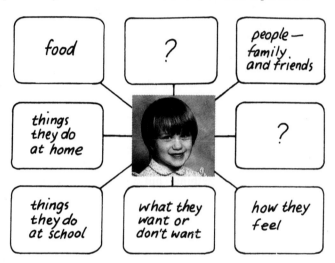

The next stage is to identify what the children use language for in each of these areas, that is to say the language 'functions'.

Stage 2: What does a child use language for in each of these areas?

Each of the areas in stage 1 can be explored further. The suggestions here are not intended to be exhaustive but to give the general idea of the language functions within one area.

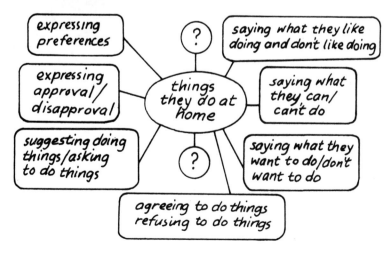

We also need to consider whether the child is most likely to need to be able to use language in these areas in the form of speaking, listening, reading or writing. There are some things which we read or write far less often than we hear or say them. For example, children are most likely to be speaking when they are asking to do something. It is important to remember this when you are structuring your own programme because it means that any reading and writing exercises on these areas are really only for the purpose of checking and backing up learning rather than for promoting real language use. So, reading and writing activities for them should be kept in proportion. Similarly, a quick glance at the topic above will also show that this particular area of language as a whole is more concerned with the language they will *produce* than the language they *receive*. In contrast, the topic of things they do in school will contain a large proportion of language that the children have to understand but not necessarily produce. So, in each case, you would want to bias your teaching accordingly.

Stage 1 was to identify some of the areas of the children's lives which are most relevant to them. Stage 2 was to think about the language needs they have in those areas. The final stage is to identify key concepts, key vocabulary and key structures which can provide a starting point for those areas in another language. Remember, we are only determining a starting point at this stage. Of course we would like the children to know more than one way of 'suggesting doing something', but one way will be enough to get them started.

Stage 3: Choosing starter phrases/vocabulary/structures

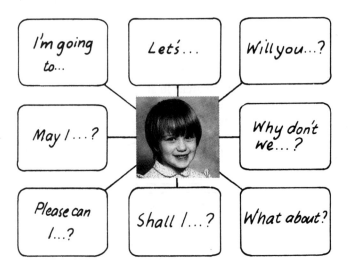

This is a rather rough and ready system but it works and you can refine it as you go along in the light of experience. Having generated some initial ideas like this, you can set out the product of your thoughts in a form which looks more like a programme or syllabus! So, the ideas so far begin to look like this:

TOPICS	FUNCTIONS	KEY PHRASES	SKILL
1. Activities at home	i) suggesting things to do / asking to do things ii) saying what they like doing / don't like doing iii) expressing preferences iv) expressing approval / disapproval v) saying what they want to do / don't want to do vi) agreeing to do things / refusing to do things vii) saying what they can / can't do	Please can I ... Let's ...	Speaking

It will not only help you and the children to have something like this worked out, but it will also enable you to pass on to the next teacher a summary of what the class has done.

It is not difficult to work something like this out for yourself, but this is also a very suitable topic for an inservice workshop or just for informal discussion with a friend or colleague. More importantly, this is a key area in which the teacher can involve the children in the decision making process and give them some responsibility for their own learning. After all, one of the priorities identified earlier was to help the children develop a feeling that the language is for them to use. You can make a considerable contribution to 'making it theirs' by involving them in the process of selecting the content of their programme, if you are free to do so. It will also help their learning in two other ways.

- If they have thought the programme through in some way with you, they will know where individual bits 'fit'.
- They will have an 'investment' in what you are doing and a greater commitment to working with you to make it successful.

**5.3
Involving the
children in the
planning**

If you are their class teacher, the best occasion for working out the programme with the children would probably be in their mother tongue classes before they start the foreign language. If you only meet the children for language classes, you could do the exercise with them at the beginning of the year. Note that in the process of setting up the language course with you in this way, they will begin to discover a great deal about how language and communication work generally. In most countries, this is an important part of mother tongue classes. So, in this way, the foreign language programme is already supporting other aspects of the children's development and learning and is becoming integrated into the overall curriculum. At the same time, by setting up a programme which clearly matches the way they use their mother tongue, you are also establishing very clearly that all languages are equally about real people communicating. The foreign language is as normal as their mother tongue but different. The concept of different normalities is a vital one for our children to grasp in the multicultural, multilingual communities of today.

One possible way to set up this mother tongue introduction to the language programme is as follows:

- Tell the class that you are all going to think about what they need to learn in the foreign language and that you are going to start by doing a survey together of what kinds of things they talk about and how they talk about them in the mother tongue. Get them interested in the idea of finding out what people actually do talk about. Discuss whether and in what ways it is different from what they read or write about. The weather is a good topic to get this point across. For example, we rarely describe weather except in writing (holiday postcards). We usually comment on it ('Isn't it hot'). Weather forecasts have their own way of talking ('Sunny with occasional outbreaks of rain'). Children already have a sense of appropriateness. They would recognise the absurdity of chatting about the weather in the style of language used in a weather forecast, even if they couldn't express it. It may need to be articulated and explored. Try too to help them recognise that they don't all use the mother tongue the same way. For example, do they all have the same words for meals? (English children don't, as anyone knows who has tried to sort out the complexities of lunch/dinner/tea/supper.)
- To shape and record your discussions and explorations with the class, you could use the 'spiderchart' approach with them, just as the previous pages suggested you could use the charts to help yourself. So, for example, you could start by pinning a large picture of a child to the board and by getting the children to start suggesting which topics are of most concern for someone of their age. It will perhaps help if you start from concrete examples. Get each child to write down three things they have talked about this morning to their family, or three things they have talked to their friends about since they came to school. Again, by working like this and by introducing the children to the spiderchart, you are doing more than just setting up the foreign language programme. You are introducing them to a way of exploring, collecting and collating their own ideas. It is a strategy that you can introduce again on many other quite unrelated occasions such as class discussions of problematic issues, or pooling ideas for the next class outing. We need to help children to articulate ideas as well as to have them.
- Once they get the idea of identifying topics and building up a chart, let the children work out their own stage 1 chart in pairs. When they have done that, you can build up a class version on the board around your picture.

There is no need to rush this process. Remember, you are not just getting the children to give you a list of possible topics as quickly as possible. You want to encourage them to explore how they and others use language. So, for example, you can discuss the inclusion of certain topics which one pair suggests. Is there any agreement on what the main topics are? Get the children to clarify what they mean by the topics. If they say 'sport', are there some sports and not others which they would include? They could (in the mother tongue) do class surveys of the kind suggested in *Practical Activities 1*. They would then be familiar with the process when they encountered it in the foreign language lesson. If you are their class teacher, you can also help them process the results in their maths work in the form of bar charts or pie charts.

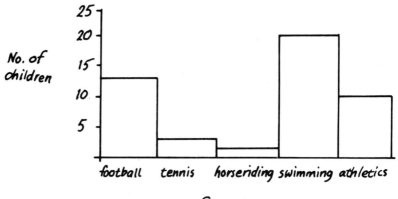

In this way, you can help the children to work through the various stages of the 'spidercharts'. For example, after they have identified food as a topic, you can take them on to what sort of things they say in connection with food, what sort of food language they read and hear, and what kinds of food are most common in the class. (Another good topic for a class survey.) By working through the approach with them, you can develop a framework on which you can be seen to have based your programme when they start the foreign language work.

Having looked at one method of choosing the content of your own programme, the next question for teachers who are responsible for designing their own programme is how often in the week they should offer language lessons and how long these lessons should ideally be.

**5.4
Deciding how frequent and how long language lessons should be**

Here, as in so much else to do with teaching, there is no clear cut answer. However, if you have any part in deciding the time allocation for language teaching, you need to know the relative merits of the various possible patterns of work. Briefly, they can be summarised as follows.

More than an hour of high density language work at a stretch is probably too much for most teachers and their classes. Less than half an hour is very insubstantial and fragmented. This sets the parameters. Within those, if you have roughly two hours a week to spend explicitly on language work, you can choose any combination of hours/half hours you like. By having four half hours, you can spread the contact through the week. The advantages of this are:

– The children do not lose sight of the language between sessions. It does not need reestablishing each time, but becomes an expected part of nearly each day, just like maths and science.
– The children have more chance of remembering work from one session to the next.
– You can deal with a few simple things each lesson, without 'losing' a class with a short concentration span.
– You will probably appear to get through the work more quickly because more frequent lesson endings seem to encourage us to finish things off!

The disadvantages are:

– Frequent lessons probably take more total preparation time than the equivalent amount of time needed to prepare two large blocks.
– Short lessons can be very demanding for both teacher and class. In order to do something worthwhile in a short session, teachers often find themselves putting in a great deal of emotional and physical energy as a stimulus to get things moving.
– Shorter lessons offer much less space for the children to do their own thing in worthwhile interactive or independent activities.

The advantages of two longer lessons are:

– It is easier to undertake sustained work on a topic without the thread being broken.
– You do not have to spend so much time recapping at the beginning of each lesson.
– Longer lessons may demand more ingenuity in planning, but they encourage us to make economic multiple use of our prepared materials and therefore can actually take less time to prepare.
– In longer lessons, we are more likely to leave children the space to process things for themselves and, by the same token, give ourselves a bit more breathing space.

The disadvantages of longer lessons are usually seen to be:

– They are more likely to present behaviour problems.
– They are more difficult for the inexperienced language teacher initially. (Remember, however, that there are ways discussed in Chapter 3 of reducing these potential problems.)

So, there is no clearly preferable approach in planning the frequency and duration of language lessons. As with so much in teaching, it is a matter of identifying the advantages and disadvantages of rival systems and deciding which advantages you yourself want and which disadvantages you can cope with.

This chapter and the preceding one have discussed language programmes and patterns of work. In doing so, they have, for the moment, been looking at language work as a freestanding 'subject', which is how it usually appears in schools. There is a danger here. If we only offer the children language work as something separate in this way, it tends just to be something the children do with and for the teacher. Yet we want to encourage them to perceive and experience another language as something that they personally can use. That was one of the priorities identified in Chapter 2. It was suggested then that one of the best ways to make a language real is to use it for other learning. So, whether you are working fairly closely with a coursebook or whether you are free to create your own programme, it is important to look for ways, however modest, of integrating language work and other learning. The next chapter looks in detail at possible strategies.

6

Integrating language work and other subjects

Is this Maths work?

. . . Or English?

This chapter deals with three aspects of integrating languages and other subjects:

– why it is a good idea;
– what makes it possible even with young learners at a early stage of their language work;
– ideas for how it can be done.

Practical Activities 2 (pages 143–169) then provides detailed suggestions of how to put these ideas into actual practice in the classroom.

6.1
Why is integration a good idea?

We have already seen earlier that it is important for the children to see the new language they are learning as something normal and natural. It should not therefore be something set apart from the rest of their learning. They should see it as something to use, not just something they manipulate in language classes. Furthermore, recent language acquisition theory stresses that one very powerful way we 'get hold' of a language is by receiving and producing real messages. So, learning other things in English will help children to learn English. In the process, they will be handling real meaning rather than just words and structures for their own sake.

There is also a third, more pragmatic reason for integrating language work and other learning. Both teachers and learners benefit from bringing existing skills and understanding to bear on new areas and from encountering familiar ways of working when meeting an unfamiliar focus of teaching or learning.

Even if there are at least three good reasons for trying it, most teachers initially find the idea of integration rather unrealistic. They either doubt their own ability to do it or they think it will be too difficult for the children. However, as this chapter intends to show, there are forms of integration which are worthwhile without being too complicated and difficult for either the teacher or for the children. This is because there are several key elements which language work and other school learning have in common.

6.2
What makes integration a realistic possibility?

If you compare the work you do in language lessons and the work you do in other lessons, you will find that however different the content of the lessons, in certain respects they build on the same processes.

In particular, those processes are:

– diagrammatic representation of information;
– repeated pattern;
– understanding through seeing;
– responding by doing.

It is these key elements in common between the subjects which will help us to integrate language work and other learning even with learners in the early stages. It is therefore worth looking at them a little more closely.

Diagrammatic representation

A diagram or chart enables us to handle complex information more easily and concisely than we can through straightforward text. For example, if railway timetables were written out in continuous sentences, they would be almost impossible to read. A diagram can also show relationships and significance more clearly than can the written or spoken word alone. The chart on pages 114–115, for example, enabled us to see the implications of our answers about the advantages and disadvantages of a coursebook much more clearly than if we had just answered the questions without setting them out diagrammatically.

Children encounter diagrammatic information in all subjects. In maths and science particularly, they are themselves encouraged to learn how to express and read ideas diagrammatically. The illustration at the beginning of this chapter is a good example. The children are asked to read the words and draw in the appropriate picture. So, for example, in one column they draw a small cat and then a tall cat. Or they might work across the diagram and draw in a small cat, then a small girl, then a small boy, etc. The exercise was originally a mother tongue maths exercise designed to teach children the concept of coordinates. In fact, it works equally well in the early stages of English as a reading exercise which demands an active response.

This is because language classroom work also builds on activities which carry and record information in chart form. The grids in *Practical Activities 1* are another example. So, clearly, the handling of information in this way is an element common to other subjects and to language study and can clearly provide one starting point for integrating the two types of work.

The role of repeated pattern

The second starting point is the role of repeated pattern in all learning. Pattern is fundamental to understanding and learning. It is the way we store information in our brains. It is the way we make sense of the physical world about us. Patterns and observation of pattern are central to maths and science.

Pattern is also the way we make sense of language. Our sense of grammar is a sense of pattern. That is why small children produce regular but wrong forms of verbs such as 'I eated', 'He goed'. It is why they can form plurals for words they have never met before. Good language activities exploit this sense of pattern. So here too is a common starting point.

Understanding through seeing

Seeing as a source of understanding is central to language work. This is because we do not just take meaning *from* language. We get hold of a great deal of our mother tongue by taking meaning *to* language. If we understand the message, we start to understand the language. If we understand the language, we get the message. There is a kind of reciprocal and mutually reinforcing relationship.

We understand the language.   We understand the message.

But, unlike the proverbial chicken and egg, we do in this case know which comes first; understanding the message, since this happens before we have any active language of our own. Something other than language must carry messages. That something else is what we see, hear and feel going on around us. In fact, seeing as a key source of understanding is not just an element of language learning and acquisition. It is an element of all good teaching. Again, science and maths work make particularly full use of seeing in order to understand. Here then is the third shared element which gives us the potential for integration.

Responding through doing

Even in our mother tongue we do not always respond to language with language. Sometimes this is because just doing something is itself the most appropriate response to a language message we have received. After all, if someone asks us to open the door for them, it would be odd to say 'I will open the door for you'. We simply do it. However, physical response is also one of the ways in which we handle partial understanding. By allowing the other person to see what we do as a result of what they said, we soon discover whether we have interpreted the message correctly. Besides, we can often understand more than we can articulate. For this reason, good teachers make room for non-verbal response in all subjects. In the early stages of language learning, when the ability to articulate is a long way behind the capacity for understanding, responding through action has a particularly significant role to play.

So, not only does integration seem a good idea, but we can also see that there are common elements between language lessons and other lessons which will help to make it work. The next and most vital question, therefore, is what we can actually do in practice to encourage integration both in outward events and in the children's minds. It is, of course, always possible to slip little bits of English into other work. You can, for example, include an occasional English poem in mother tongue classes. Or you can teach the children an English song when it is time for music. Similarly, it is not difficult to do simple sums with English numbers. But we are looking for something more substantial than this, whether it be for teachers who only teach languages or for teachers who are also class teachers and therefore already teach other subjects.

We can look for ways to:

– use work from language classes as the basis for work in other lessons;
– take techniques which the children are learning in other subjects and use them to promote language work;
– use topics from other subjects in language lessons;
– teach other subjects wholly in the target language.

6.3
Using language classes to provide material for work in other lessons

In maths, children are going to learn at some stage to record information diagrammatically. They will be making pie charts and block graphs to show distributions and correlations. They normally do this with information gathered from various class surveys showing, for example, how far from school the members of the class live, likes and dislikes, who has what pets, and so on. Usually, these surveys are conducted in the mother tongue as part of the maths lesson. Some of them, just as easily and far more usefully, can be done in the language lesson. After all, the interview grids suggested on page 68 are designed for the class to use in order to find out about each other's preferences, possessions and circumstances. Although their purpose is to practise certain questions and answers in the foreign language, they are an eminently suitable source of the material needed for the maths lesson. So, what better than that the children do the survey in the foreign language class and use the results to apply their maths?

For example, in the language lesson, the children are learning the transport phrases 'by bus, by car, by train, by bike'. As a final activity on this topic, the children conduct class interviews. Each child interviews twelve people using the question 'How do you come to school?' The child records the results in note form, for example:

How do you come to school?

Name	by bike	by bus	by car	by train	on foot	other
1 Rita		✓				
2 Carlo	✓					
3 Giovanna		✓				
4 Rebecca			✓			
5 Tommaso				✓		
6 Andrea	✓					
7 Cristiano	✓					
8 Claudia					✓	
9 Franca					✓	
10 Elena						taxi
11 Michele		✓				
12 Pietro	✓					
Total 12 =	4	3	1	1	2	1

Later, in the maths lesson, the children arrange the information they have collected by turning it into a pie chart.

Or, a similar language questionnaire of a survey on pets could be turned into a block chart.

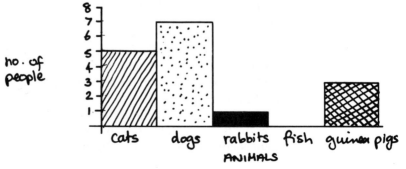

By using the language lesson in this way to provide material the children need for their other work, the language work is being tied in with the rest of their learning and the language itself is being tied in with thinking. It is therefore doubly real language use.

6.4

Using techniques from other subjects to stimulate language work

This second example also builds on the same features of diagrammatic representation and repeated pattern. This time, the teacher has identified the mathematical concept of intersecting sets as a good basis for meaningful language repetition. At about the age of six, English primary children start in their mathematics work to handle the concept of sets and, later, intersecting sets. In the diagram below, we have two intersecting sets within the universal set of the class 2B.

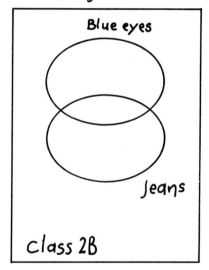

There is a set of those children who are wearing jeans and the set of those who have blue eyes. The maths teacher would be asking questions in the mother tongue like:

'Who in the diagram is wearing jeans?'
'Who has blue eyes?'
'Who has blue eyes and is wearing jeans?'
'Has x got blue eyes?'
'How many children have blue eyes but are not wearing jeans?'
'How many children are not wearing jeans and have got blue eyes?'

In mathematics, the teacher would be stressing the key words 'and', 'or' and 'not' (what the mathematicians call the 'logical connectives'). This is not very different from what a language teacher would be asking. With very little alteration, this could become a basic language activity. For example, one possibility is to use the diagram as a chart which the children have to fill in as a listening exercise, for example, on the topic of food:

TEACHER: David likes fish but he doesn't like cheese.

The children write 'David' in the appropriate place on the chart.

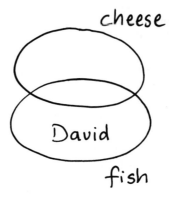

The sets could be based on the perennial topics of pets, hobbies, likes and dislikes, and so on. We could also achieve greater variety by using more than two intersecting sets. For example, this is how the diagram could look if you wanted to use it for meaningful practice on 'hobbies'.

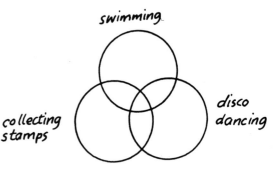

Another basic technique, this time from science, which transfers to language work is that of 'sorting'. Here is a diagram from some science work for young children.

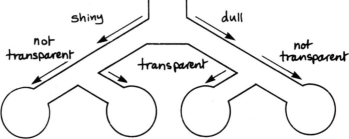

It was part of a series of activities in which the children were learning to sort objects into categories. In this case, they were sorting sweets according to whether they were dull, shiny, transparent or not transparent. They did this by moving the sweets down the pathways, choosing the route according to the sweets' characteristics. This sorting and categorising process is an important part of the children's intellectual development. It later becomes more complicated and more abstract. In a language class, we can help to develop that same intellectual process by applying it in language practice as this next worksheet shows. We would again be linking language and thought in a very real way.

Children's worksheet

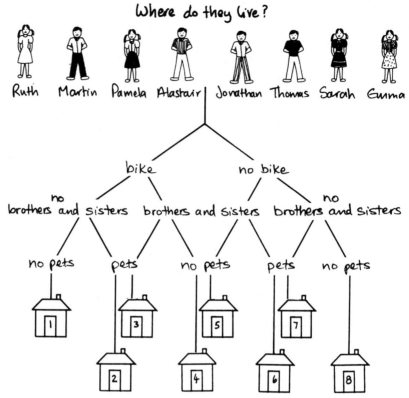

Where do they live?

Teacher's textsheet

Can you find where they live?

Ruth has got a bike. She has one brother and two sisters. She has got a cat.	Martin hasn't got a bike. He has no brothers and no sisters. He hasn't got any pets either.
Alastair has a bike. He has no brothers or sisters. He has a dog called Bess.	Pamela has a bike. She has no brothers or sisters. She has no pets.
Emma hasn't got a bike. She has a sister called Ros. She has a cat called Fluffy.	Jonathan has a bike. He has two brothers. He has no pets.
Thomas hasn't got a bike. He has no brothers or sisters. He has a goldfish.	Sarah hasn't got a bike. She has five brothers. They haven't got any pets.

137

6.5
Introducing topics from other subjects into language lessons

We need to provide children with as much understandable listening as we can. Some of the best possible listening activities in the language classroom are those where children are listening to a commentary about something they are watching and are therefore processing both the new and the familiar language in the light of what they understand through seeing. This is a major source of indirect learning. The idea here then is for the language teacher to increase the integration of language work and other learning by doing a mini-demonstration in the language lesson of something which ties in with work to be dealt with later in a mother tongue lesson. So, for example, if you or another teacher are going at some stage to talk to the class in science about the way different substances expand at different rates, you can precede this in the language lesson by a brief demonstration and commentary on how to take a tight metal lid off a glass jar by submerging it in water.

This is not a complicated laboratory experiment which needs special equipment, a special room or even special language. You only need a jam jar with the lid screwed on very tightly indeed, a thermos of hot water and a small bowl. At this stage, all you are doing is providing the children with something interesting to watch while they listen and something which can provide the starting point for further work later in the mother tongue. The lesson would sound and look something like this:

TEACHER'S WORDS	TEACHER'S ACTIONS
We are going to do an experiment.	*Have your carrier bag of 'equipment' on the table.*
Now, watch carefully.	
Here is a jar.	*Hold up screwtop jam jar.*
I am going to open the jar.	
. . . Uh . . .	*Exaggerate the effort required.*
I can't open the jar.	*Try again.*
Peter, can you open the jar?	*Pass the jar to one of the children.*
He can't open the jar.	
Gill, can you open the jar?	*Pass the jar round the class.*
No, she can't open the jar.	
Who is going to try? Miranda? OK. Can you open the jar? No.	*Various children try.*
So, how are we going to open the jar?	
Watch.	

TEACHER'S WORDS	TEACHER'S ACTIONS
We are going to use a bowl and some hot water.	
Karin, can you find the bowl in the bag?	*There is no guarantee that the child will pick out the right thing!*
Ah, you've found a biro.	
OK. Give me the biro. Now, can you find the small round bowl?	*Show 'small', 'round' with your hands.*
Thank you.	
Now Michael, can you find the hot water in the bag?!	
It is in a thermos flask.	
Yes, that's right. Thank you.	
Now, *(to the rest of the class)* watch.	
Michael is going to put some water into the bowl.	*Show 'pouring' motion with thermos and bowl.*
Be careful, it is hot!	
Just a little water.	*You don't want too much water in the bowl or it will overflow when you put in the jam jar!*
Now, Karin is going to put the jar into the hot water.	
Good.	
Now we are all going to count up to thirty. Can you count up to thirty? One . . . two . . . three . . . etc. Now. What is going to happen?	
Take the jar out of the water.	
Now can you open it? . . .	

When you begin the 'proper' science lesson in the mother tongue, you can start by saying 'Do you remember what happened? What did we do? What happened then? Why do you think . . . etc.' as you normally would.

Again, language has been used for a real learning experience and the follow up lesson can provide a very natural crosschecking of understanding between the mother tongue and English, which is a far cry from 'translation' or demanding exact equivalents.

6.6 Teaching whole lessons of other subjects in English

There is little doubt that being educated through the medium of the language you are learning is the best experience of real use of that language that schools can provide. However, few if any of the teachers reading this are likely to want to, or be organisationally able to teach large parts of the curriculum in English. What is being suggested here is much more modest, namely that you sometimes teach whole lessons in other subjects in English. This approach has its own advantages. For example, it allows you to set the foreign language event within a supportive mother tongue framework. Perhaps in a series of primary science lessons on the body you will want to include at some stage a lesson on the way in which our pulse rate changes after exercise. This is exactly the kind of strongly visual and active lesson which is suitable for teaching in English. By putting the lesson in English between two mother tongue lessons on the general topic, you will be able to do three things.

- You can introduce the topic and the general approach in the mother tongue in the lesson before. So, in this particular example, the children will have spent the previous lesson discussing the overall theme of the body and fitness, devising tests and doing trials with breathing rates after exercise. They will also have been told that in the next lesson they are going to investigate the pulse. In this way, they come to the Science-in-English lesson knowing what procedures to expect and already knowing what words like 'pulse' and 'heartbeat', which they are about to hear in English, must mean.
- You can discuss fully in the mother tongue afterwards (in the final session) the significance of the events that the children have participated in during the Science-in-English lesson.
- You can thus leave the middle session free to concentrate on demonstration, action and data recording in English. In this way, you are building on the four elements of diagrammatic information, repeated pattern, understanding through seeing and responding by doing.

It is not a problem for teachers to find suitable topics like this to teach in English. After all, there are plenty of strongly visual and active topics in primary science alone. However, for most people, the worry is that the whole event is too complicated both for us and for the children. This does not have to be the case. In fact, teaching a whole lesson of another subject in a foreign language is in many respects simply a sustained combination of already known techniques and approaches. For example, for most teachers, a lesson on the way our pulse rate changes with exercise would probably involve some combination of:

- showing the children how to take their pulse;
- getting the children to record their pulses before and after exercise;
- recording the results;
- writing a record of what they did on a worksheet such as the one opposite.

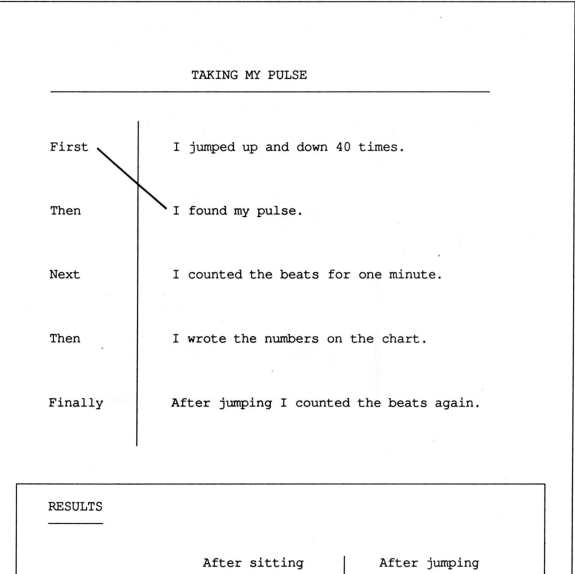

TAKING MY PULSE

First   I jumped up and down 40 times.

Then   I found my pulse.

Next   I counted the beats for one minute.

Then   I wrote the numbers on the chart.

Finally   After jumping I counted the beats again.

RESULTS

	After sitting	After jumping
MY PULSE RATE		

Each part of such a lesson on its own asks for fairly simple and probably already familiar techniques for teaching in English. For example, showing the children how to take their pulse can be along the lines of the stage by stage demonstration and simple commentary described in the 'jam jar' activity. Getting the children to do the practical work involves the same process as making the 'fortune teller' on pages 72–74. Showing the children what they have to do in the written work is based on the same principle of 'explaining by doing' as we saw in Chapter 2 (page 16) for setting up pairwork through the target language. The actual writing up of the experiment itself is based on a fairly common language teaching technique of matching up two parts of a sentence. These processes are written out in detail in the next section, but it should already be clear that teachers do not really have to find new communication skills in order to teach in English. They merely have to make more deliberate use of existing ones.

This chapter has looked in general at the ideas and basic processes behind integrating language learning and other subjects. The final section, Practical Activities 2, now shows in detail various ways you can set up such work in the classroom.

Practical Activities 2

Introduction

It is one thing to think of interesting things to do in the classroom. It is not always so easy to work out manageable and effective ways of doing them. This section therefore takes the examples from the previous chapter and variations on them, and shows stage by stage how you can put them into practice. As before, however, these remain *suggested* procedures to give you an idea of what you might do. They are not a prescription. The topics too are only examples. You will find different but similar possibilities in your own syllabuses.

You will notice how the activities and the suggested procedures build on the four elements of diagrammatic representation, repeated pattern, understanding through seeing, responding by doing. These are the basis for this kind of integrated work whatever topic you choose.

At the same time, the activities in this section have not lost sight of the priorities, principles and practical considerations on which the activities in Part I were based. They are, of course, particularly good examples of real language use and indirect learning. Some of them demand language risk taking from the children but do so within a secure framework which promotes confidence. These activities also exploit the children's capacity for interaction and talk. They build on the children's capacity to work meaningfully with limited language. Whilst having a very serious underlying purpose, they have also not lost sight of the children's capacity and need for play and fun. Finally, they, like the previous activities, have 'stirring' and 'settling' qualities as well as degrees of 'involvement' which we have to take into account when we set them up.

The examples are grouped under the four approaches suggested in the previous chapter:

1 Using language classes to provide material for work in other lessons.
2 Using techniques from other subjects to stimulate language work.
3 Introducing topics from other subjects into language lessons.
4 Teaching whole lessons of other subjects in English.

GROUP **1**

Using language classes to provide material for work in other lessons

Activity **1**
English→maths

This example shows class surveys followed by diagrammatic representation of the results. It is a simultaneously involving activity which builds on the children's desire to talk to each other. It also provides them with a good reason to get out of their seats.

Language focus in this example

Months.

Materials required

You need an interview chart for each child, as in the example below. It has been adapted slightly from the grid format suggested previously in order to make it easier to do the mathematics afterwards.

Name	J	F	M	A	M	J	J	A	S	O	N	D
Total												

Preliminary work

– It is better if the children are already familiar with the months of the year and with the question 'When is your birthday?'
– Set the scene in the previous maths lesson by telling the children that you are going to conduct a survey in the English class so that you can use the results in maths.
– At the beginning of the English lesson, remind the children that you are going to do a survey for maths. (It may seem trivial to state the obvious like this, but remember that the whole point is that the children themselves see the integration, not just us.)

Suggested procedures

– Write the first letters of the months on the board and give the class a
little repetition and accuracy practice in saying them. (Write them up so
that you can draw the chart round them later.)

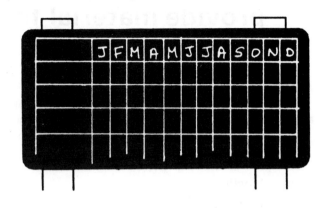

– Now remind the children of the question they will need:

TEACHER: My birthday is in July. When is your birthday, Anna?
ANNA: December.
TEACHER: Paul, when is your birthday?
PAUL: April.

– Draw the chart framework round the prompts.
– Interview a couple of children yourself, filling in as you go.

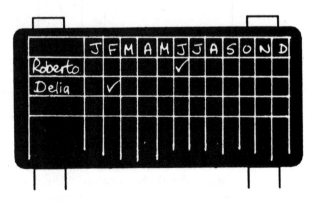

– Do a third interview, this time getting one of the children to ask the
question and fill in the answer on the board.
– Now the class are probably ready to start on their own. Issue the charts
to the class or get the children to draw their own.
– Let the children move around the room interviewing each other.

After they have finished, collect in the charts so that you do not have to rely on the children keeping them safe until you need them in the maths lesson. In the maths lesson, you can then show them how to draw their own chart like the one below.

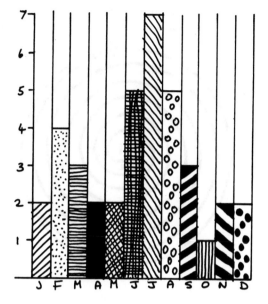

Final comments

i) This is an integrating activity which you can use even if you are not a class teacher and therefore only see the children for language lessons. There is no reason why you should not do the follow up maths charts in your language class if you want to, although if you are in a position to coordinate what you do with the class's other teachers so much the better.

ii) There is only one quick question and answer in this example so it will not take the children very long to interview the whole class if necessary. If the survey had more than one question, they could ask fewer people, but remember that they need a big enough sample to make a worthwhile chart.

iii) It does not have to be a pie chart or a block graph. Why not get the children to devise their own way of recording the information they have discovered?

Activity **2**
English→science

Practical Activities 1 suggested an activity which involved the children in making a 'fortune teller' (page 72). Following English instructions like this in order to make something is both meaningful and fun. Here is an activity based on the same principle, which is even more meaningful because the children are making something which they will use in their science lesson. They are going to make spinners in preparation for science work on colour.

Language focus in this example

General practice in following instructions.

Materials required

– For each child a spinner sheet like the one above (and one or two spare sheets in case someone makes a mistake).
– String, thin cardboard, scissors, glue.
– Felt tips if the children do not have their own.

Preliminary work

No special preliminary work is required by the children, but do try this out yourself first so that you can spot potential difficulties. You will then have an example to show the class what you are all going to make.

Suggested procedures

– Give out the spinner sheets.
– Show the class step by step what to do:

Stage 1: Colouring the first disc

TEACHER'S WORDS	TEACHER'S ACTIONS
Choose two colours.	*Chooses two felt tips.*
Now, watch carefully.	
Take one colour, . . .	*Takes one.*
and find the number one.	*Looks obviously for the small number on the disc.*
Start here.	
Follow the path carefully! . . .	*Colours in the path, doing a little bit, then showing the class, then a little bit more.*
. . . .	*Lets the children do theirs.*
Now, take the other colour, . . .	*Repeats the procedure.*
and find the number two.	
Start here.	
Follow the path carefully! . . .	

Stage 2: Colouring the second disc

The children colour the second disc the same way (either with the same two colours or with another two). You can then continue the 'telling by showing' demonstration:

– Cut out the discs roughly and stick them onto thin cardboard.
– Cut round them neatly and stick the discs together back to back.
– Make a hole through the two hole marks with a sharp pencil.
– Cut a piece of string approximately 90cm in length and thread it through the two holes and tie the ends together.

The spinner is now ready. To make it work, loop the string over your forefinger, twist the spinner a few times. Then pull and relax the string alternately. This makes the spinner rotate and you can see the colours mixing.

This activity leads into the science topic of exploring colour mixing.

Final comments   i) You might find it more convenient to make the spinner (in English) in a handicraft lesson, in which case you will have achieved three-way integration!

ii) Even if you do not follow up the activity in science, it is fun to do. It integrates language and handicraft, and it provides meaningful language listening practice just by itself.

Activity **3**
English→PE

If you would enjoy doing something more energetic and unconventional, how about getting the class to make up its own 'disco routine' to do in the PE lesson?

Language focus in this example

Parts of the body and physical actions.

Materials required

– A tape recorder and a tape of dance music.
– Paper for the children to write on.

Preliminary work

As before, this is a consolidation of work they have already done.

Suggested procedures

– Remind the children of the parts of the body. Use a variety of action words like 'shake', 'roll', 'stamp', 'point', 'bend', etc. To begin with, they can just obey the instructions by copying you. Then you can play the traditional game of 'Simon Says' where the children obey your instructions ('Shake your left hand.') only if you first say 'Simon Says'. Start with the class standing up. When they make a mistake they have to sit down.
– On the board write up your disco routine.

- Do the routine with the children in time to your chosen music.
- Now get the children to make up and write down their own routine of four actions in pairs. Go round and help them.
- Get each pair to write their names on the top of the paper and collect the papers in so that you can check if there are any major problems.

In the PE lesson, you can start with your own routine briefly to reestablish the idea, but then hand the children's own papers back and get pairs of children to teach their classmates their own dance routines.

Final comment

Again, it is possible for you to do this activity entirely in the language lesson if that is the only time you see the class. But if you do it in an ordinary classroom, you will need understanding neighbours. Perhaps the best place for it is outside on a summer's day!

GROUP **2**

Using techniques from other subjects to stimulate language work

Activity **1**
Intersecting sets as a listening exercise

Chapter 6 discussed how handling information in diagrammatic form allows children to work with quite complex ideas without us asking them to read or write anything complicated. Such activities also come in the category of 'settlers' as they involve all the class physically and mentally at the same time.

Language focus in this example

Food.

Materials required

The children need something to write on, either their books or some rough paper.

Preliminary work

As a listening activity this can come very early in the introduction of the topic because it requires recognition of the words and not production.

Suggested procedures

Stage 1: Showing the children what to do

– Draw three intersecting circles on the board and identify which food each circle represents.

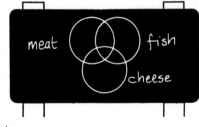

– Make a statement:

'Angela likes fish and cheese. She does not like meat.'

– Write 'Angela' in the appropriate place, making it clear as you do so that you are working it out:

'Angela likes fish so her name is . . . er . . . here. Wait a minute. . . . She likes cheese too, so . . . here. Ah, but she doesn't like meat so . . .' etc.
– Do one or two more examples yourself so that the children get the idea.

Stage 2: Making sure the children understand what they have to do
– Now make another statement.

'Tom likes cheese. He doesn't like meat and he doesn't like fish.'
– Get one of the class to come to the board and show everyone where to write the name.
– Do this several times.

Stage 3: Over to them!
– Once the children have got the idea, get them to draw their own intersecting circles.
– Read out a series of statements like the examples above. Each child fills in their diagram with the information you provide.
– At the end, check back using your board diagram so that they can see where the answers should be.

Possible follow up/Variation

'Listen and move to the right circle'

This is an alternative if your class is small and you have use of the school hall or if it's a fine day and you can use the playground. It is a rather more physically involving version of the above listening activity. The sets can be marked by large, different coloured, chalk circles on the ground. (If you would like to try this activity with a large class, you could subdivide them into smaller groups, each with its own set of circles.) The children organise themselves according to the teacher's statements. For example:

TEACHER: Stand in the red circle if you like meat.
Stand in the green circle if you like cheese.
Stand in the yellow circle if you like fish.

Notice that the children will have to move and rethink their position as more information becomes available, i.e. if they like meat, they will first go and stand in the red circle, but if they also like fish, they will have to move to where the red circle overlaps with the yellow circle.

Other language you can practise with this activity	Any 'sets' you wish to combine. You can make these all on one topic, e.g. colours: 'X is wearing red and blue but not green.' Or you can use this as a revision activity to recombine various areas of work already done, e.g. 'Y plays football, has a bike, and likes discos.'

Activity **2** **Intersecting sets as a speaking activity – a variation on 'Battleships'**	In *Practical Activities 1* (page 64) there is a version for the language classroom of a game called 'Battleships'. In the traditional game, each child has a matrix of squares on which they secretly block in certain squares representing their 'fleet'. The children have to guess where their partner has located the ships on the matrix. We have already seen that you can adapt this activity to the language classroom by identifying the coordinates with phrases rather than numbers. Diagrams of intersecting sets lend themselves to the same kind of work. The procedures are exactly the same as those on pages 64–67, but instead of the children having grids on which to mark their choices, they have diagrams of intersecting sets and an agreed set of names.

Child A marks in her choices on her diagram but keeps them hidden so that Child B cannot see.

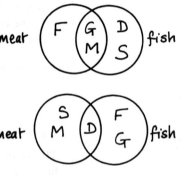

Child B does the same.

The children take it in turns to guess where the other's choices are. For example:

CHILD A: Fiona likes fish. She does not like meat.

A hit is scored so . . .

CHILD B: Yes.

Now it is Child B's turn to guess what is on Child A's diagram.

Activity **3** **Sorting as a listening activity**	We saw in Chapter 6 that the basic skill of sorting and logical categorisation was one of the areas where language work and science conveniently overlap. It was suggested that the basic sorting diagram could become a logical listening exercise using the sheet opposite.

Children's worksheet

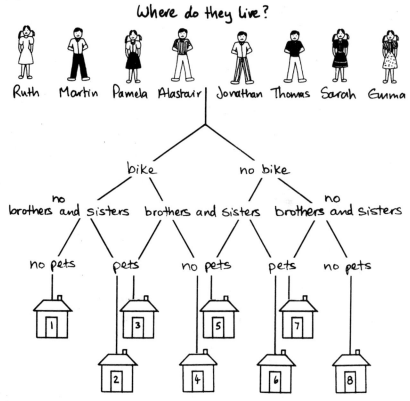

Where do they live?

Ruth Martin Pamela Alastair Jonathan Thomas Sarah Emma

bike   no bike

no brothers and sisters brothers and sisters no brothers and sisters

no pets   pets   no pets   pets   no pets

1   3   5   7

2   4   6   8

Teacher's textsheet

Can you find where they live?

Ruth has got a bike. She has one brother and two sisters. She has got a cat.	Martin hasn't got a bike. He has no brothers and no sisters. He hasn't got any pets either.
Alastair has a bike. He has no brothers or sisters. He has a dog called Bess.	Pamela has a bike. She has no brothers or sisters. She has no pets.
Emma hasn't got a bike. She has a sister called Ros. She has a cat called Fluffy.	Jonathan has a bike. He has two brothers. He has no pets.
Thomas hasn't got a bike. He has no brothers or sisters. He has a goldfish.	Sarah hasn't got a bike. She has five brothers. They haven't got any pets.

155

Language focus in this example

Personal details.

Materials required

A copy of the children's worksheet on the previous page for each child or pair of children and your textsheet.

Preliminary work

The children should have heard the words before and should be able to recognise them, but as a listening activity, this can come quite early in the sequence of work on a topic. Remember that the activity is part of learning the words. It is not just something they do after they have learnt them.

Suggested procedures

Stage 1: Showing the class what to do

– Give out the worksheets and let the class look at them. Now make sure they have put their pens down because, for the moment, you want them to watch not write.
– Hold up a copy of the worksheet so it is facing the class. Read out a description of one of the people at the top of the sheet. At the same time, slowly trace the information path with your finger, making it clear that you are making a choice about which way to go. For example:

TEACHER: Ruth has got a bike.
She has one brother . . . and two sisters.
She has got a cat.

This will bring you to house number 3, so show the class that you write in 'R' for Ruth on the door.
– Repeat the same set of information, but this time the class trace the path with you and write 'R' on their own sheets.

Stage 2: Go!

– Read out three statements about Martin. Watch out for any children who are still looking unsure. One or two may still need help at this stage. Check by glancing round that they have put 'M' on the correct door.
– Now that the pattern is established, the children can match all the people with their houses in the same way.

Other language you can practise with this activity	You can use the standard sorting pattern for any topic you like, for example, names and physical characteristics. In this version, the children have to fit a name to a description.

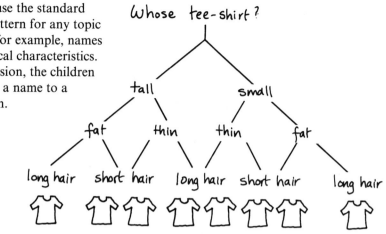

Activity **4**
Sorting as a reading exercise

This activity is probably only suitable for older primary children. Once the children are used to the sorting pattern as a listening exercise, you could set them the task in pairs of working out the diagram from the information they are given. The worksheet would look like this:

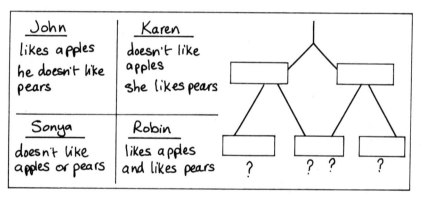

The children would complete it like this:

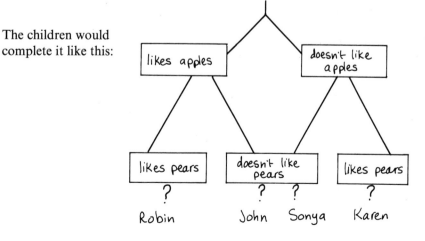

157

GROUP **3**

Introducing topics from other subjects into language lessons

Activity **1**
Maths→English: Measuring

Chapter 6 described an experiment with a tight fitting jam jar lid. It showed how a science topic, in this case the topic of differential expansion rates, could provide meaningful listening practice in a language class. This present example shows how a topic from maths can provide equally meaningful and at the same time more active work in a language lesson.

Here is an example of some measuring work done by two eight-year-old English primary school children in their maths lesson.

It took Michelle 3 seconds to run 10ms

It took Clare 3½ seconds to run 10ms

It took James 5¼ seconds to run 10ms

It took Mick 3 seconds to run 10 ms.

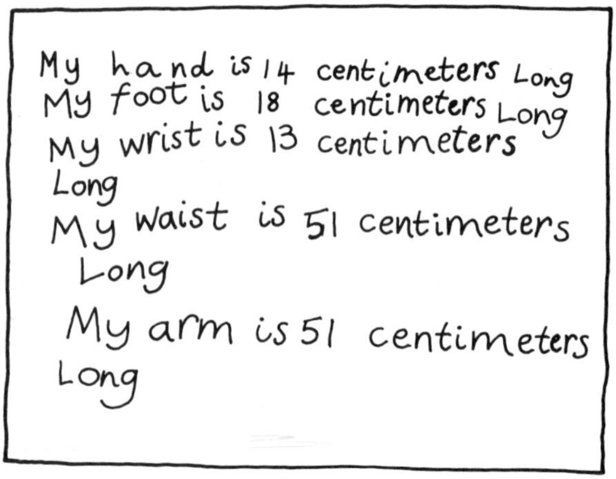

My hand is 14 centimeters long
My foot is 18 centimeters long
My wrist is 13 centimeters long
My waist is 51 centimeters long
My arm is 51 centimeters long

We can see immediately that although the two children were concentrating on learning to measure and record measurements, the work produced very simple and repeated language patterns. This is exactly what we are looking for in language classes. So, how could we use it? Here is one suggestion for language work based on maths measuring work.

Language focus in this example

Concepts of height/width/length.

Materials required

Whatever measuring equipment is to hand.

Suggested procedures

Stage 1: Showing the children what to do

– Measure something at the front of the room (perhaps the teacher's desk) while the children watch. Or get a child to measure it for you.
– Record the results on the board in English:

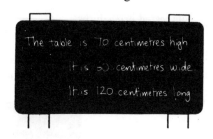

The table is 70 centimetres high
It is 50 centimetres wide.
It is 120 centimetres long

Stage 2: Collecting information

– Get each child to measure five items in the room. They should note the measurements down in rough and then write them neatly in their books in full sentences like the ones on the board.

Stage 3: Extending the language work

– Borrow one child's book and read out some of their results to set a 'riddle':
'It is x centimetres long, y centimetres wide and z centimetres high. . . . What is it?'
– You could then encourage each child to make up a riddle for their classmates based on two or three of their objects.

Possible follow up

After you have led the class through some of these oral riddles the children can write up their own riddles and put the answers upside down at the bottom of their page.

Final comments

i) Notice that in this kind of work the children are not just practising the words, but are also getting to grips with the concepts of height, width and length.

ii) It is also interesting to note in passing that one of the English children, whose written work we saw on the previous page, was still exploring the use of these words in the mother tongue. In fact, she has got it wrong. An adult would not say that someone's waist is 'long'. If children are making mistakes like this in their mother tongue, it is a salutary reminder to us not to expect children who are working in a foreign language to get everything right.

Activity **2**
Maths→English:
Comparisons

You could do a similar exercise on the basis of comparisons. The concepts of 'bigger' and 'smaller' are familiar work in most maths programmes. In our language classes, we have to teach children comparisons. So we can take the maths topic and turn it into a combination of language work and thinking as follows.

Suggested procedures

Stage 1: Showing them what to do

– Start by measuring several children and recording the results on the board in a way which makes the language pattern clear, for example:

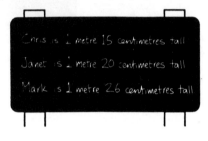

Stage 2: Developing the language work

– Start discussing the comparisons:
  'Chris is taller than Janet. Is that true?'
– After several examples, get the children to ask the questions.
– Write up a sample statement and question.

Stage 3: Setting the children to work on their own

– The children each measure three friends of their own if, of course, you have actually got the necessary equipment for them to do this. If not, you do some more measuring and the children copy your table of measurements from the board. They then write their own statements and true/false questions. Again, they can put the answers upside down at the bottom of the page.

GROUP **4**

Strategies for teaching whole lessons of other subjects in English

When it comes to teaching a whole lesson of another subject in English, the main concern of most teachers is not the topic of the lesson but the language required. This last section on integration therefore concentrates on just that. How can we sustain a whole lesson in limited English? This example comes from the lesson on the pulse in Chapter 6. If you remember, the lesson takes place between two mother tongue lessons on the topic and its structure is as follows.

A Science-in-English lesson

The teacher is going to show the children how to take their pulse. The children are going to record their pulse rate before and after exercise. The children are going to record how they did the experiment.

Language focus in this example

Developing the children's ability and confidence in working with partial understanding.

In the lesson extracts which follow, notice how the teacher's language and behaviour help the children to understand what is happening, even though they do not necessarily understand every word. Watch, too, for ways in which the teacher reinforces and builds on patterns of language. For example:

– Notice how the teacher shares the structure and inner logic of the lesson with the children so that they have a general sense of what is going on.

LANGUAGE	HOW IT HELPS
She uses simple, emphatically spoken marker words like:	These small words give the children important messages like:
Right . . .	We are about to begin.
OK . . .	We've finished that bit.
So . . .	This is what we're going to do.
Good . . .	Everything is under control!
Now . . .	This is an important bit to understand.
Next . . .	See how this connects with what we've just been doing.

N.B: These words are all followed by short pauses which emphasise their importance.

161

– Notice too how the teacher provides a path of 'stepping stones' through the meaning. She makes sure that there are enough bits for the children to understand easily, so that even when they do not know everything that is happening, the children are not getting lost. The teacher emphasises, repeats and rephrases. She supports words with gesture and demonstration and sometimes writes them up on the board.

LANGUAGE	HOW IT HELPS
Keywords for action	
Listen . . .	These words give the children the
Watch . . .	security and confidence of knowing
Wait . . .	what they are supposed to do, even
Write . . .	if they are not 100% sure of all
No! . . .	that is being said.
Do this . . .	
Don't do that! . . .	
Like this . . .	
Keywords for today's subject	
Pulse.	You will be able to relate these
Pump.	words to the mother tongue lesson.
Blood.	Meanwhile, they are learning real
Chart.	language attached to new
	information and ideas. Life is not
	all pets, food, colour and weather.

– Finally, notice how at the same time as she is helping the children securely through the lesson, the teacher is providing language practice. The children hear repeated patterns in speech and writing, for example: 'Can you . . .?' 'We/You are going to . . .'.

The teacher also provides additional comments (but as asides, with less emphasis and less volume), which the children don't need to understand but which they can begin to understand because the general meaning is clear. In this way, the teacher builds up their skill in partial understanding and their ability to pick up language because they already understand the message.

To summarise:

In the extracts that follow, look for: marker words;
keywords;
repeated language pattern;
gesture and demonstration;
supplementary language.

Finally, alongside the lesson, there are comments written in the margin to remind you of the points made at the beginning of the book about young learners and our priorities.

One word of warning. This kind of detailed description becomes very slow on the printed page and there is a risk that it makes events look more complicated than they are. It will help if you can give it life by imagining a class of children with their teacher.

Suggested procedures

Stage 1: Setting the scene and showing what is going to happen

TEACHER'S WORDS	TEACHER'S ACTIONS	COMMENTARY
Now . . . watch carefully.	*Pauses, catches their eyes and looks keenly at them for a moment to signal something important is about to happen.*	These pauses are very important. Notice the marker 'Now' and the keyword 'Watch'.
Can you find your pulse?	*Puts own fingers in position.*	Beginning of repeated pattern.
I can feel my pulse. Bip . . . bip . . . bip. That's my pulse.	*Makes pushing gesture with hands to show beating. Points to word on board.*	Supplementing and extending language.
Can you find yours?		Repeated pattern.
First take off your watches.	*Takes off watch.*	Marker – 'First'. Understanding through seeing and responding by doing.
You are going to find your pulse.	*Points to word.*	
Now, do this.	*Catches their attention again and demonstrates.*	Marker.
Like this . . .		Understanding through seeing.
Put your fingers like this.		
Three fingers. 1 . . . 2 . . . 3. . . . Here, by the bottom of the thumb.		Extending the language.

TEACHER'S WORDS	TEACHER'S ACTIONS	COMMENTARY
Yes, that's right.		Responding by doing.
Michael? Rita?		
Now, press gently like this. Can you feel your pulse?	*Demonstrates.*	Marker. Repeated pattern.
Can you feel it beating? Bip . . . bip . . . bip. . . .	*Looks round while talking to check that all the class are looking confident.*	Repeated pattern.
Can you feel it? I can feel mine. It's going bip . . . bip . . . bip. . . .		Repeated pattern.
My heart is pushing my blood round my body.	*Gestures to heart and makes action of pushing.*	Extending language backed by understanding through seeing.
Push . . . push . . . push . . . bip . . . bip . . . bip. . . .	*Checks while talking that the class look as if they are understanding, and gestures with each beat.*	
It is pumping the blood.	*Points to word on board.*	Subject words coming out by gesture, words on board and emphasis.
I can count it. 1 . . . 2 . . . 3 . . . 4 . . . 5 . . .		Repeated pattern.
Can you count yours, Henry?		Responding by doing.
Good.	*Looks round.*	
June?		Checking understanding without being explicit.
Good.		Notice that the teacher does not say 'Do you understand?'.
Can you all feel your pulses?	*Looks round very carefully.*	

TEACHER'S WORDS	TEACHER'S ACTIONS	COMMENTARY
OK. Now, (the next question is) how do we measure it?		Doubling of markers as you move on to the next stage.
(Yesterday we measured our breathing rate.) How are we going to measure our pulse rate?		This is language they don't have to understand but are beginning to process. Remember, they know from previous mother tongue lessons that you are going to measure.
	A child points to the stopwatch, another child says 'clock' in English, a third child says 'stopwatch' in the mother tongue.	Note the mother tongue/ English mix. It is what you expect in these lessons. It is part of creativity with limited resources, and will encourage risk taking. The mixture also allows children at different linguistic stages to participate equally in the lesson.
Right, we are going to use the stopwatch to measure our pulse.		Repeated pattern – 'We are going'.
Now, watch.		Keyword – 'Watch'.
I am going to measure mine.		Notice we are getting a very natural switch between 'I/ you/we', which is very difficult to produce in language exercises.

Stage 2: Measuring and recording normal pulse

TEACHER'S WORDS	TEACHER'S ACTIONS	COMMENTARY
Ready?	*Looks round.*	Marker.
Watch.		Keyword.
First, here is the stopwatch.	*Holds up stopwatch.*	Marker followed by pause and showing the sequence.
I am going to set it. Like this. See ? . . . 30.	*Makes all actions just a little larger than life so they are clear.*	
Then I find my pulse.	*Demonstrates searching for and finding pulse again.*	Searching round for the pulse as if unable to find it will reassure those children who do not find it straight away.
Ah . . . . Here it is.		
Start the watch now, Keith.		
I can feel it. 1 . . . 2 . . . 3 . . . 4 . . . 5 . . . 6 . . . etc. 41 . . . in thirty seconds my pulse rate was 41.	*Counts.*	Repeated 'I can'.
I am going to write it down.		Repeated 'I am going'.
I'll write it here.	*Demonstrates on own worksheet by writing in the information and holding it up for the class to see.*	Keyword – 'Write'.
Right.		Loud, emphatic marker and big pause to show a new stage is about to start.
Now you are going to do it.		Repeated 'You are going'.
Ready? Wait.	*Makes stop gesture.*	Keyword – 'Wait'.
Are you ready, Jason? Marion?	*Looks round the class obviously, acknowledging individual children.*	Notice it is important in these lessons for the children to feel you are with them, not cut off by the language.

TEACHER'S WORDS	TEACHER'S ACTIONS	COMMENTARY
Count in your head, silently (without saying anything, so we can't hear).	*Gestures.*	Supplementary aside.
Go!		
How many, Gary? Emma?		
Write it on your paper, here.	*Points, checks round.*	Responding by doing.

Stage 3: Jumping on the spot and taking the pulse again

This stage continues in the same way.

TEACHER'S WORDS	TEACHER'S ACTIONS	COMMENTARY
Now we are going to jump.	*Demonstrates.*	
We are going to jump 40 times.	*Writes 40 on board.*	
Stand up.	*Gestures.*	Responding by doing and understanding through seeing.
Ready?		
Go!		
1 . . . 2 . . . 3 . . . 4 . . . count with me! 6 . . . 7 . . . 8 . . .		The counting also provides a chance to speak!
Sit down.	*Gestures.*	
Quickly find your pulse.	*Demonstrates.*	
OK?		
Quiet.		
We are going to measure the pulse again.		Repeated pattern with the new language.
Count in your head.	*Gestures.*	
Go!		Responding by doing.
Write it down on your paper . . . on your chart, here.	*Demonstrates on own chart.*	Understanding through seeing and responding by doing.

Stage 4: Writing up the procedures on the worksheet

TEACHER'S WORDS	TEACHER'S ACTIONS	COMMENTARY
OK . . . Good! Now . . . What next?		Lots of markers and pauses for the transition. They also serve to calm a class down.
You are going to write what we did.		Keyword and supplementary language.
Watch.	*Holds up worksheet so it's facing the class.*	Keyword – 'Watch'.
What did we do first?	*Points to where the worksheet says 'first'.*	This 'is it this one' approach is a standard procedure worth developing in other language activities too.
'I jumped up and down 40 times.' Is that it? Is that the first thing?	*Points to and reads out one sentence.* *Gestures '1' with finger.*	Repetition of 'First'.
Or 'I found my pulse?' Yes? . . . No!	*Points to another sentence on the sheet.* *Obviously searches.*	Understanding through seeing.
Ah . . . . Here it is . . .	*Makes clear she has found it.*	
'I took my pulse for 30 seconds.' Can you find it?	*Points to the right sentence on the worksheet.*	
Look on your paper.	*Looks round to see who has identified the correct sentence.*	Responding by doing. Again checking without drawing attention to it.
Good. Now (you are going to) join the two (parts of the sentence) like this.	*With a thick, black felt tip, the teacher draws the line between the two matching parts of the sentence and holds it up for the class to see.*	Supplementary language in the form of an aside the children do not have to understand.